Build Your Wealth

The Path to Financial Freedom and a Rich Life

Learn how to earn more, save more, and live an abundant life. A step-by-step guide to a Luxury Lifestyle

©Written by Steven Marshall

Copyright © 2020 By GLOBSELL. All Rights Reserved Worldwide.

No part of this publication may be reproduced or transmitted in any form without the prior written consent of the publisher.

Limit of Liability/Disclaimer of Warranty: The publisher and author make no representations or warranties with respect to the accuracy or completeness of these contents and disclaim all warranties such as warranties of fitness for a particular purpose. The author or publisher is not liable for any damages whatsoever. The fact that an individual or organization is referred to in this document as a citation or source of information does not imply that the author or publisher endorses the information that the individual or organization provided.

Tabel of Contents

INTRODUCTION 6

HISTORY OF MONEY 9
SPENDING HABITS BASED ON AGE 10
GENERATIONS THROUGH TIME 11

CHAPTER 1: DEFINING WEALTH AND FINANCIAL FREEDOM 15

WHAT IS WEALTH? 15
WHAT IS FINANCIAL FREEDOM? 19

CHAPTER 2: THE FAST WAY TO BUILD YOUR FINANCIAL FREEDOM AND BE DEBT FREE 26

HANDLING YOUR STUDENT LOANS 30
PAYING OFF YOUR HOME FASTER 33
ADDITIONAL STEPS TO HELP YOU ACHIEVE YOUR GOALS 34

CHAPTER 3: GETTING RICH AND BUILDING YOUR WEALTH 53

HOW TO GET RICH: BOLD MOVES THAT WILL GUARANTEE WEALTH 53

CHAPTER 4: DIFFERENT INVESTMENT STRATEGIES AND START INVESTING 62

UNDERSTANDING INVESTMENT 62
BRIEF HISTORY OF INVESTING 63
TYPES OF INVESTMENTS 63
HOW TO INVEST MONEY WISELY? 65
THE PRIMARY ASSET CLASSES YOU CHOOSE ARE BASED ON THE RISK .. 71
SET A DEADLINE AND CHOOSE AN INVESTING GOAL 73
INVESTING GOALS YOU SHOULD CONSIDER 74
DEFINE YOUR INVESTMENT BUDGET 75
INVESTMENT STRATEGIES 77
INVESTING TIPS 87

CHAPTER 5: WAYS TO HANDLE YOUR MONEY WHILE INVESTING 88

DECIDE ON HOW MUCH HELP YOU NEED 88
SET GOALS AND DEADLINES 89
CHOOSE YOUR INVESTMENT ACCOUNT TYPE 90

OPEN YOUR ACCOUNT 91
CHOOSE YOUR INVESTMENT STRATEGY 92

CHAPTER 6: BEST WAYS TO SAVE MONEY FASTER IN A MONTH 94

STOP RELYING ON WILLPOWER 95
BE REALISTIC 96
PAY YOURSELF FIRST 96
AUTOMATE YOUR SAVINGS 97
EXAMPLES OF WAYS YOU COULD SAVE CASH WITH LESS EFFORT 99
EXAMPLES OF SOME EASY WAYS TO SAVE ON YOUR EXPENSES 102

CHAPTER 7: SETTING UP A HIGH-INTEREST BANK ACCOUNT FOR FREE WITH NO SET-UP FEES 109

WHAT ARE SOME BENEFITS OF BANKING ONLINE? 109
WHAT TO CONSIDER AND TO SET UP YOUR ACCOUNT 111

CHAPTER 8: NEGOTIATING LATE FEES, HAVING A PLAN, AND HANDLING CREDIT CARDS 113

TALKING YOUR WAY OUT OF FEES 113
AVOIDING LATE FEES 116
HANDLING CREDIT CARDS 117

CHAPTER 9: OUTSOURCING TO VIRTUAL JOB AND ALL YOU NEED TO KNOW 119

VIRTUAL JOBS 119
HOW MUCH WOULD A VA TYPICALLY COST, AND IS THAT THE BEST CHOICE? 128
HOW TO WORK WITH A VA? DO THIS! 132
HOW TO WORK WITH A VA? DO NOT DO THIS! 137
RESPONSIBILITIES OF A VA 140

CHAPTER 10: WAYS TO TRAVEL MORE WITHOUT QUITTING YOUR JOB AND STILL BE FINANCIAL STABLE 154

PRIORITIZE IN FINDING A FAST INTERNET ACCESS 154
EMBRACE WORK AND PLAY AS THE SAME 155
RESEARCH PLACES TO WORK 156
BE CLEAR WITH YOUR MANAGER OR CLIENTS 156
BE WISE ABOUT HOUSING 157
PLAN YOUR TRAVELS AROUND PAID HOLIDAY WEEKENDS 157
TAKE SHORTER TRIPS DURING THE WEEK TO MAXIMIZE YOUR VACATION TIME .. 157
THINGS TO AVOID 158

Reasons Why You Do Not Need to Quit Your Job 160

CHAPTER 11: HOW TO ACHIEVE THE LIFESTYLE YOU DESIGNED 163

Decide on What You Want Out of Life 164
Start to Envision Your Life is Already How You Want It 165
Think About the Experiences that Make you Happy and Repeat Them 167
Become Goal-Oriented 168
Forget the Past 169
It Does Not Matter What Everyone Else Thinks 170
Let Go of Fear 172
Communicate Your Wishes with Others 173
Steps to Attract the Life You Want 174
The Path to Begin Designing Your Lifestyle 182
The Best Way to Create a Vision You Want in Life 185

CONCLUSION 190

Introduction

Are we getting anxious every month with bills, subscriptions, and memberships? Living paycheck to paycheck? Having only enough to live? No savings? Perhaps these are the questions that transpire in our lives most often or maybe every month after getting your paycheck. Some of us even question ourselves if we ever get to see the day, we are debt-free. Almost all of us are living a life only to achieve monetary gain to pay dues. We spent half of our years paying off debts, maybe even more, regretting that we are not doing what we want. This is the burden of a financially dependent person. Almost everything revolves around money.

Everyone has a dream of financial freedom. We investigate our futures and wonder what they hold. So many people continue to pay the bills such as the mortgage, auto, utilities, and loans; yet, they are still in debt. Perhaps they have student loans or credit cards. When you pay the minimum balance on these bills, you are only paying the interest and a small amount of the principle. No wonder you will never get out of debt. It keeps piling up. It seems like you can never get ahead. Sometimes it feels you take one step forward and are push three steps back. Here is the secret, *"you are not alone."*

Most people think paying only the minimum will keep them content. This is great if you want to stay in debt. However, you probably did not wake up this morning telling yourself, *"I want to stay in debt."* Therefore, what do you do about your debts?

Maybe you want to do more than just get out of debt. You are encouraged to put away some money for savings. Wait, why stop there? This is a crazy idea, try building your wealth and establishing your financial freedom for your family. You can ensure you never go into debt again.

Throughout this book, I will show you step-by-step on how to obtain your financial freedom. Do not let the banks, bills, and debts control you. It is time to regain control.

You are about to take an adventure of earning money, saving money, and living a life of luxury. Keep in mind, a life of luxury does not mean you will be the wealthiest person in the world. Although, that would be a great goal. Make sure your goals are attainable but set them high.

Do you enjoy traveling? I love to travel. The problem is the job. You need to work to survive. You are living from paycheck to paycheck and conscious about how you spend your hard-earned money. When this happens, it is hard to travel. As you follow the steps within the next few pages, you will start to see the stability you need. Eventually, you begin to see your wealth begin to increase. You are now out of debt and have stayed out of debt for over a year. You still see the money rolling in. Think about all the money you are saving from being debt-free. Is it not a great feeling. You can finally go on that trip you always wanted. The best part is you do not need to quit your job to do it.

Many years ago, I found myself with over $10,000 in debt. I could never see the bottom of all the liabilities. It was a struggle. I did not know what to do. I had credit cards, student loans, a mortgage, etc. The list goes on and on and on. It was so hard that I could not pay some of them, and it negatively affected my credit score. When this happened, it made it very hard to get another credit card, buy a new vehicle, or invest in a home for my family. Lenders did not trust me. My credit report shows I am not responsible. It was not until I found the secrets to financial wealth that things started to get better. Those secrets are in the following pages.

There are no secrets in getting out of debt fast. However, there are tricks to helping you get there faster. It takes time and dedication. I will also show you a few easy ways to help you grow your wealth and stay out of debt.

We are about to embark on a quest together with the goal of you being free from debt and finding your financial freedom. It is time for you to experience the benefits of growing your wealth.

You may have heard the famous phrase, *"Money does not buy happiness."* Money does, indeed, buy happiness if done in the right way. Most often than not, having less money becomes the source of a lot of pain, frustration, and anger, while it consumes your life, and sometimes ruins relationships. When we do not have money, our problems seem to be about money.

History of Money

Money is only an object. It can be a shell, a rock, and a piece of paper with printed faces on it. The value that people are putting on it makes it different from other things. Money is a medium of exchange, a measurement for someone's wealth, and a form of payment.

Money was a part of history about 3000 years ago; however, before that, people use to swap goods or services as their primary source of exchange. Bartering is a direct trade of objects or services without using money. For example, I will give ten livestock in exchange for ten sacks of food. It can be anything as long as the two-individuals agree to the terms.

However, bartering has its disadvantages. It took a long time since you have to find the person suited for what you are looking for and vice versa. It does not have a standard measure of value as it is difficult to store for wealth since most of it is perishable. After that, the Chinese used actual tools and weapons as the medium of exchange around 770 B.C.

The tools were difficult to carry, and so they decided to turn them into a metal circle-like shape, creating the world's first coin. Then they moved to paper money, just around 700 B.C. The faces printed on the paper suggest the denomination. After that, the European banks started using banknotes for their clients, and they would exchange these notes to buy goods. They then operated like the currency does today.

The only difference from the banknotes and today is the notes were made by the banks, not the government. The government took care of all the money and created the world's capital. Throughout history, the value of paper money has remained as the primary medium of exchange until the rise of the 21st Century, wherein mobile payments and virtual currency begin. This method provides convenience and comfort to people, eventually replacing the paying of goods and services with cash and create a cashless system. Technology slowly designed a world that is far different from our history. Yet, the bottom line is **money**, despite the many advances, still has a positive and permanent effect on how people are living today.

Spending Habits Based on Age

As we go through history, it is essential to know how each generation spent money. The different spending habits will enlighten us based on people's age. This will shed some light on which production has a harder time controlling their finances. It will also bring factors that can contribute to our reasons why we need to be more financially independent. You will see what the appropriate age to start saving for your future or perhaps to begin investing is. Therefore, while the medium of exchange or money changes over time, so makes the spending patterns of consumers.

As consumers age, both their level of spending and how they allocate their budget varies. Even so, when the so-called *"life events"* happen, such as getting your first job, getting married, having children, and even retirement will contribute to the ways people spent their money.

Generations Through Time

Throughout time, we have been faced with new generations. Each one is specific to that time. As times changed, so do these generations. It is essential to understand how these have changed over time. By understanding how each generation is, will help you understand the needs for you to obtain financial freedom.

The Greatest and Silent Generations: Anyone born before the year 1945 is part of this generation. People were aging from the '70s to 75 years old. They are called Greatest and Silent, for they spend less than any generation. It is common for people to pay less as they grow older. They do not have to commute since they are not fond of getting out and spent less on expenditures, and they stay at home most of the time. The value of money had become less for they are interested in valuing life more, and intangible things are worth more than money. However, health care and retirement are two factors that are higher in getting paid by these types of people.

Baby Boomers: Baby Boomers are those born between 1946-1964. They used to make up most of the population of the United States until the Millennials came along. They spent most of their shopping time online; thus, this generation is often the focus of marketing campaigns and business plans as they are big spenders. Their spending habits reflect their values and priorities, such as eating healthy foods, spending on pets, and housing expenditures. They are regarded as hard-working individuals who value family relationships most of the time and spend money on food gatherings and special occasions. They put importance to positivity above all else. They are close to retirement years and allocate most of their budget on their retirement plan. Yet, some of them are still on the workforce, because they are not done with paying debts.

Generation X: This generation is dubbed as the *"forgotten or overlooked generation."* They were born between 1965 to 1980. Bring them to be older than Millennials but younger than Baby Boomers. They have the most considerable disposable income. They shop more conservatively than Millennials, and they will not be won over by some flashy advertising or celebrity endorsements. They prefer honesty and personalization. They buy more from face-to-face shopping and excellent customer service. They are not into technology and only rely on the younger generation to help them navigate the online shopping world. They do their transaction through cash most of the time.

Millennials: This is the modern generation and progresses along with technology. They are born in the year 1981 to 1996, aged roughly 22 years old to 32 years old. This generation is guilty of wasting more money than any other generation. They are called *"the nation's biggest spenders."* Most of these people had less than enough savings, and some of them don't have savings at all. Their purchase habits are influenced by their instincts or by their peers; most of them are buying retails, which are significantly branded.

However, they are picky when it comes to price and value discounts more. They follow brands for discounts and promos. Yet, they spend money over perishable things such as coffee, gadgets that are only available for a limited time, clothing, and eating out. Most of these individuals do not have credit cards or car loans since banks had tightened their requirements. They are fond of using online transportation bookings, such as Uber or Lift. They also enjoy monthly subscriptions, such as online movie streaming, television, music, etc.

Overall, this generation is already on the working force giving them more opportunity to buy their needs with monetary value. They feel superior in their finances, thinking they are underpaid, yet this generation had at least a small motivation to save money. Some of them do not have savings or even invest in something more valuable for the long-term. They are recognized as spenders rather than savers.

Generation Z: This generation is born after the year 1997. The eldest of this demographic are on their way to graduate college or to enter the workforce. This generation differs significantly from another aging period in terms of saving, spending, and overall allocation of their money. Since they are born during the era of technology, they have access to almost all the information they need before making a decision, making them smart shoppers. Online access makes them more informed about things that allow them to strengthen or learn new entrepreneurial skills. Despite their young age, these people engage more in business than any other individual.

They are more self-reliant and independent, which is because they grew up in a digital world. Online statements made by other purchasers efficiently pursue individuals who belong to this group as they rely more on the excellent review and efficient service in buying goods.

Knowing and going about each age and their spending habits tells you that money makes up the whole personality of a person. According to their age, they spend their budget based on their impulses. Most people who belong to the modern-day group have low regard for saving money. Therefore, knowing the basics and essential part of learning how to gain Financial Independence and gives you a fighting edge.

Chapter 1: Defining Wealth and Financial Freedom

We all want to be out of debt, have financial freedom, and grow our wealth. Before we can start to build our wealth and achieve these things, we need to understand what that means.

We will be exploring the world of personal financing and slowly take the steps towards achieving our goal of gaining Financial Freedom. We will walk through the steps towards our objectives. We will enumerate them and reside in each stage to further contemplate the idea. I will be explaining the history of Finance, ways on how people have been using monetary means over time, spending habits according to age, and learn techniques on how to become financially independent.

What is Wealth?

Having wealth does not always mean money. Wealth has many different faces. You could have wealth in personal growth, developing more meaning to your life, and a relationship with your family: spouse, children, and parents. However, in today's world, most people still look at it as having a lot of money. Wealth is more than just money; it is things your money cannot purchase. Wealth can be the simple things in life that we enjoy. These are things you want to do and bring you pleasure and satisfaction.

An example of having wealth is Donald Trump. He has a lot of business ventures, property, and money. However, my favorite example is Jeff Bezos. Bezos is the wealthiest person in the world. He is the founder of Amazon and has remained the CEO since 1994. We all know of Amazon and how big the company is. He started from nothing. There is a saying, *"You have to spend money to make money."*

In 1994, Bezos probably had a lot of debts. Like any business venture, there will always be debt. He worked hard to grow his wealth and become debt-free. His next step was to have the financial freedom he longed. Through his passions and desires, he continues to develop his wealth until his net worth in March 2020 was $113 billion.

Most people view wealth as money and will put it into three categories.

- Protect Capital – This means you want to stay productive.
- Grow Capital – This means you are not done, and you want to get richer.
- Enjoy Capital – You worked hard for your money and now can enjoy it.

These are great. However, there are four types of wealth that we can use to categorize the wealth you have.

- Financial Wealth – This means the money you need for you to keep you enjoying the thing that pleases you is where the other three categories fall.
- Social Wealth – This means your status with your friends, family, and those you associate with all the time.
- Time Wealth – This means having more time to do things that you enjoy.
- Physical Wealth – This means your physical health factors. For example, you go to the gym, for a walk, and eating healthy.

As you can see, we tend only to see one-fourth of the wealth you have. The hardest one to achieve is Financial Wealth. Therefore, we will focus on it the most, but do not forget about the other three if you want to make the ultimate wealth.

Brainstorm and think about different ways we can build wealth. I will briefly give you a few ideas to get you started. As you continue to read, I will go more in-depth on a few of the different ways and introduce a few more that will help you to grow your wealth.

You should create a budget: Creating a budget is an excellent start to building your wealth and reaching your goals of financial freedom. Through a budget, you can ensure you are on the right track.

Start paying off all your high-interest debts: High-interest debts are hurting your future. When you make the minimum payment on high-interest debt, you are paying about 85% to 90% towards interest. That means you are only paying about 10% to 15% towards the product. No wonder it takes so long to pay off your home or a new car. Instead, start making an extra payment on top of the original amount and call the company. This way, that additional cash will be recorded towards the principle only and not interest. This will start lowering your payments and getting your debt paid off faster.

Start to establish an emergency fund: At some point, you may be faced with an emergency. It is good to have a little money set aside for those emergencies. So many people do not plan for the unexpected. When they find themselves in a situation that needs the money, it is out there. Do not find yourself in these situations.

Invest your money: When you have extra money, try investing it. This is one of the quickest ways to build your wealth. If you like risks, try investing in the stock market. For those who do not like risk, you can invest in bonds. There are so many ways to invest your money. Keep in mind, the higher the risk when you invest, the greater your return.

Find ways to cut back on your living expenses: You can find extra money through your living expenses. Start looking at your budget and where your money goes. You will notice certain areas where you can cut back on and not spend so much.

Learn to negotiate your salary with your boss: It does not matter if you are just getting hired or have been with a company for years. You can still settle your salary.

Start building your wealth in your 20s: Most people start getting close to retirement and then realize they need to set aside money for their retirement. Why wait? Start in your early 20s. As you put away your money early, it will start to build over time. You can slowly watch your wealth grow.

Each of these areas focuses on bringing you closer to living the luxury lifestyle you desire. The goal is to bring you wealth to do things that will make you happy.

What is Financial Freedom?

Financial Freedom has enough savings, financial investments, and a budget to afford the life you are living in. It is having the independence of money rather than the other way around. It is having control of your expenses and practicing financial management for your benefit and your family. It means growing your savings fo retirement earlier than you planned, being financially prepared in any emergency, and pursuing the career you love without being driven by your salary. It is making life decisions without having money as a significant hindrance. You are not in a pile of death. Generally, financial freedom is about dominating your finances, not the other way around.

Imagine your life being debt-free? Think of the feeling of relief with paying all your dues and not worrying about what will happen after the payments made or where you will find the next amount. Imagine making a decision that involves money without putting too much thought into it. Imagine a place that money is not a significant stressor in your life. Find the thought of you having control over your finances and having more than enough to get by. Is it great to be in a desirable place like that? Do you feel a sense of relief? This is what Financial Freedom feels like.

The freedom to choose the things you want with no worry of breaking your budget, the freedom to pay cash whenever you need to, or the freedom to retire early than planned. When you are financially independent, you start having options. You do not have to wonder whether you will be ok in the next couple of days or months. These queries and imaginable feelings can become true if you start learning how to control your finances, monitor your spending habits, and create financial goals towards achieving your financial freedom.

Not having enough cash can destroy almost everything a person has, such as goals, relationships, and even personal views. Thus, it is always essential that you know how to handle your money correctly. Making yourself aware of Financial Independence is one way to manage your wealth. There are a lot of ways to help you be better prepared in gaining independence, such as getting rid of being dependent on money. This is the most significant stepping stone towards financial freedom.

You may think wealth and financial freedom are the same. It is nice to be wealthy. However, having wealth does not always mean you have financial freedom. At the same time, having financial independence does not mean you have wealth. Therefore, we must look at wealth and financial freedom separately.

Why should you think about Financial Freedom? It sounds so easy to learn yet hard to achieve. It means that you get to have control over your finances rather than they are controlling you. You make decisions that involve money without giving too much thought of its impact because you are now prepared. You will no longer be dependent on it, and you have realized that money does not buy happiness after all. Financial Independence is a great life goal with many tangible and self-positive effects.

Having financial freedom is taking back control of your finances. You are starting to have a cash flow that allows you to have the lifestyle you desire. There are no worries about how you will pay your bills or unexpected bills each month. The debts are no longer piling up, making it hard to stay debt-free.

Sometimes your day job does not give you the extra money to establish financial freedom. You may need to use your skills and talents to work jobs outside of your day job. This may give you some extra cash flow for your savings. Overall, the goal is to have the money for retirement or a rainy day. The bottom line is financial freedom brings financial security.

Dave Ramsey has compiled seven baby steps to help you start on the right foot. I am going to briefly mention them here as we will elaborate on them further in the next few chapters.

Number one – Start your emergency fund with $1,000: You are trying to get out of debt. The goal is not to go further in debt. Therefore, to cover any unexpected expenses or emergencies, try to save $1,000 as quickly as you can and put it into an emergency fund.

Number two – Using the Debt Snowball method, you can start paying off all your debts: You do not include your home in this step. Make a list of all your mortgages, for example, student loans, credit cards, and your vehicles. Put each of them in order from the smallest to the most significant amounts. This method is known as the Debt Snowball Method. Start with the top of your list and start paying off all your debts. The smallest is at the top and should be the easiest to pay. Work your way down the list until they are all paid.

Number three – You will want to save three to six months of expenses: You are off to a great start. Now take all that money you would be paying on the debts and redirect it towards your cost savings. You will want to establish a fully funded fund for emergencies. Plain on three to six months of expenses. This means, if there is an emergency, you will have enough to survive for three to six months if you cannot work.

Number four – With about 15% of your household income, you should invest it into a pre-tax retirement or Roth IRA: What about retirement? You do not want to be still working at age 80. Most companies, unless you are self-employed, offer a 401(K). Many of them will also provide a matching program. Sometimes they match 100% of what you put into the plan. Take advantage of this. Take 15% of your total gross income for the household and put it into the companies plan. They will match it, and you now doubled your money. If you are self-employed, start a Roth IRA and deposit the money into it the same way. The beautiful thing about the companies 401(K) is the money you put into it is tax-free until you withdraw it.

Number five – Prepare for your children's college with a college fund: If you have children, you want them to have a good future. Start putting away some money for their college and invest in their future. Many banks offer individual savings accounts for college funds that have a higher interest rate to help you grow these funds. Start with your bank and see what they have to offer and start looking around and doing the research. Some banks are better than others.

Number six – You have a home, so try to pay it off early: I wanted you to save the home until very last. The reason is it usually the most significant expense you have. Start redirecting some extra money towards your home.

However, there is a trick to this. You will want any additional payments you make to go towards the principal of your home and not the interest. After paying down the principle of the house, refinance and get a lower payment each month. Now your initial payment is lower that will help take care of your interest, and you can put more towards the principal.

Number seven – Start building your wealth and give generously: Congratulations! You are now out of debt. Continue to build your wealth with all that money you have that was usually going towards debts. I will give you one more added secret that helps with this last step.

Everyone needs to do taxes on what we make. Use some of your wealth to donate to charities. The cash value of your donations is deducible on your taxes up to a specific amount. It is essential to check with the IRS to see how much that will be. It usually is around 50% of your adjusted gross income. In some cases, it may only be 20% or 30%.

These are only the beginning. The choice is yours. These baby steps are only a small glimpse into obtaining your financial freedom and creating your wealth. I am going to show you a few other ways to help you get to a luxurious lifestyle with wealth and financial independence, although I will take it a little further and discuss ways to get you there faster.

Achieving the primary goal of financial freedom is not a walk in the park. I have categorized the types of people based on their age and spending habits for us to understand the concept of saving early. We also define money as the world's medium of exchange so that we can get a better picture of how money works. Now, it is up to you to create a perfect plan to reach your goal of financial independence.

Chapter 2: The Fast Way to Build Your Financial Freedom and Be Debt Free

Everyone has some form of debt. This debt could be credit cards, the mortgage payment on your home, or a new car payment. For those who went to the university or are planning on going, you may have student loans. It seems like the debts keep coming, and there is no escape.

In the previous chapter, I talked about the Snowball Method. I am going to go a little more in detail about how this works to help you get out of debt faster. Student loans will be included in the method; however, I will add a separate section for a few details on how to manage student loans and going to school without it causing you to build up the debt. Keep in mind, your home will not be included in the Snowball Method. Therefore, I will include a section for your home. The goal is to be entirely out of debt and stay that way.

The Snowball Method

Have you ever built a snowman? When you make a snowman, you start with the base. This is the most massive ball and will hold up the rest. The next shot is slightly smaller, and the last ball in the snowman is the lowest.

The Snowball Method is Like Building a Snowman

The Snowball Method is like building a snowman. Make a list of all your debts. This does not include your regular bills like the internet, mobile phone, gas, or utilities. Those are all monthly bills and not considered debt. For example, you have student loans, credit cards, auto loans, and a personal loan.

- Student Loans: $30,000
- U.S. Bank Credit Card: $3,000
- Auto Loan (name of bank): $37,000
- Personal Loan: $10,000
- Chase Credit Card: $7,000

Looking at this list, it does not look very organized. The Snowball Method starts with getting all your debts organized. For example, we will put the most expensive debt on the bottom and start building a snowman of obligations.

- U.S. Bank Credit Card: $3,000
- Chase Credit Card: $7,000
- Personal Loan: $10,000
- Student Loans: $30,000
- Auto Loan: $37,000

Things are starting to look organized. In our example, there is $87,000 in debts. It seems a little overwhelming. I am sure you are wondering how you can get rid of this debt. Sometimes, when you have this much debt, it seems like it never ends. The more you pay on it, the bigger the debt. I am going to help you get rid of the mortgage without feeling this way.

Keep in mind, you do need to make payments on all your debts still to avoid them going to collections and affecting your credit score.

Start from the top with your debt that is the smallest amount; in our example, that is your U.S. Bank Credit Card for $3,000. If you have the extra money, pay it off in full. If you do not, start making a higher payment each month. This is your focus. Get that $3,000 paid off as fast as you can. For me, it is a smaller amount, and most people can afford to get this amount paid off quickly. You are off to a fantastic start. You already have one debt gone. How do you feel?

The next step is to tackle the next debt. You just saved a lot of money by paying off the first debt. Redirect the money you were paying for the first debt towards the future obligation. For example, you were paying a minimum payment of 35 dollars on the first debt. You figured you could afford to pay $1,000 on that debt each month. You paid it off in three months. Take that $1,000 and add it to what your minimum payment is for your next mortgage. For example, your minimum amount is $60. Now you are paying $1,060 towards the future debt if you can afford more than pay more.

For your next debt, follow the same. Redirect the money you were paying on the previous debts and add to the minimum payment of the future obligation. I think you got the idea. You can start to see how your debts are slowly disappearing. Continue this cycle until all your debts are gone. You were already spending this money on your debts, so you do not miss it. You are used to it and doing well for yourself without the cash. The great thing is how you are now making it work for you.

Congratulations! You are out of debt and did not even realize you were getting there. Your mind is now clear. You are ready to see and experience life. Take more chances to increase your wealth. Now, what do you do with the extra money? Throughout the next few pages, we will discuss different ways to handle the extra money and start building your wealth so you can obtain your goals.

I told you earlier how I was in over my head with debt. I had over $10,000 in debt. I say over, so you understand it was a lot more than $10,000. I learned about the snowball method and started to organize my expenses. I put them all in order and started from the top. Eventually, I was down to the last debt. This was the biggest one, yet, with all the extra cash, I was able to pay it off quickly. It happened before I knew what was really happening. By paying off each debt, my credit score started to go up. I was finally getting into good standings. The dream of my own home for my family and not worrying about money was beginning to come true.

Handling Your Student Loans

You just got out of High School. You have a dream of furthering your education. However, it is expensive. You may have already built up a pretty hefty student loan. I showed you how to work your investment into the Snowball Method. This is great to help you get on top of those loans. Yet, you still have not graduation and will have more student loans. Now it starts to feel like you will never be able to manage the debt. I am going to introduce a few ways that will help you go to college and not build up your debts or add to them as fast.

Scholarships: There are so many scholarship programs available. Do your research to see what is possible. You will need to apply for them based on the application process. Sometimes, you can get a full scholarship, which will pay for your education in full until you get your degree. Other scholarship programs have a set dollar amount for their award. With those with a set amount, you may need to get a student loan to cover the difference.

Grants: A grant is free money that is available to help students further their education. Take advantage of them. You can apply to them the same way as you do for your student loans. However, you do not need to pay back grants to the Government. Keep in mind, and they will not cover the full cost of your education. That means you will still need a student loan or other means of financial backing and will keep you from needing a more jumbo loan to pay for the university.

Active Military: Joining the military is a great way to handle your education and avoid student loans. They offer several programs for service members. One program that is provided is student loan forgiveness. When you join the military, you have an option for this program. It is always changing. I advise checking with the education program for more details about how to qualify.

During the time you are active duty, you can attend as much school as you want for free. The number one requirement is to maintain a passing grade. If you pass the classes, it will be covered by the military. However, if you do not give, you will need to pay for the course, and it will be taken out of your paycheck as a debt. Therefore, it still avoids having a student loan. This will give you a chance to fulfill the dream of having a degree and even become debt-free. You feel good from your accomplishments and experience the beginning of your financial freedom.

Your education will not stop there. After finishing your initial first contract, you will receive the G.I. Bill. This is used to help with your school.

G.I. Bill: There are different types of G.I. Bills. Some examples of G.I. Bills are designed for those who have been in the military. Other bills were introduced to the military after their time. My favorite is the Post 911. This bill will give you a little money to help with your housing while going to school. It is a great way to finish school as a full-time student.

The Post 911 will ensure your schooling is paid and gives you a specific amount. It is enough to pay for one degree. This is a great way to stay away from student loans.

Now, I am going to share with you a secret that will help you get out of debt faster while being a full-time student while using the Post 911 bill from the military.

You receive a stipend for your house while enrolled at the university. If you go to the classroom, you will receive the full amount. If you are doing entirely online, you will receive half of the pay. This is paid to your bank account. It does not matter if you are getting the full amount or half, it still helps pay the bills and works towards paying off those annoying debts and will give you peace of mind that after your schooling, you do not have any student loans or unnecessary obligations.

The next step is through grants. Stay away from student loans. You apply for grans and get approved. The donation is sent to the school using your Post 911 Bill. The school will receive full payment from Veterans Affairs Education for the total amount of tuition plus Books and Supplies for your classes. Once your Post 911 makes the full payment, the grant money that was sent to the school is now sent you. Use this grant money to help you get out of debt faster. It could be as much as 6,000 dollars if you qualified for the full amount.

These are only a few ideas about how to lower your student loans or not have any at all. In my opinion, joining the military, even for one contract, is the best solution and then using the Post 911 bill to help you get out of debt faster. This option is two-fold. You serve this great country, become a leader, and get an education you deserve.

Paying off Your Home Faster

You have succeeded in becoming debt-free except for your house payment. You even have a way to further your education without getting further into debt. I saved the best for last. Ok, it is usually the biggest and takes the longest.

Using the same strategies as the Snowball Method, you can work on paying your home off early. Take all that money you were spending on your debts. You do not have those debts now so we can find a good use for that extra money. You still need to add to your emergency savings. You have also already been making a house payment.

Take about 50% of what you were paying on your debts and redirect it to your house payment. This is in addition to your regular payment. Make these payments over the phone and ask them to put the money towards the principle of the home. If you only make the payment, most of it would still be applied towards the interest, and it will always take you a long time to pay for your home.

Once you pay your home down, refinance it and see if you can get a lower monthly payment and a better interest rate. This is not so you can go back to minimum payments. This is to allow the new amount due to reflect the extra fees on the home towards the principle. However, you are still going to be using the extra money to make higher payments. Instead of you paying your house off in full within 15 years, you could pay it off in 7 years or less.

The Snowball Method is one of the best ways to get out of debt the fastest. Congratulations! You are now out of debt. It is time to move on to the next step and start building your wealth. Keep in mind, and it is ok to work on building your wealth before you pay off your home. That is what the other 50% could start doing.

Additional Steps to Help You Achieve Your Goals

There are additional ways to start this journey, but it is not easy. There are no shortcuts, and it takes a big self-difference to make it work. This is a process, and it could take longer than expected, and it is crucial for you to make this journey personal. Financial Freedom must be own. Put on a lot of effort to make this journey a success.

Here's how to begin your journey to financial freedom!

Learn How to Manage Money

Did you ever wonder where your money goes after a month's budget? Did you ask yourself how you manage your paycheck each month without savings and with the same amount of debts? How did you even spend your monthly salary with no breakthrough yet still worrying about how you will get by again. You won't get ahead in life without a plan for your money. You must learn how to manage your money to get a better deal for yourself.

Imagine going to a well to get water. You lower your basket into the well and start pulling it up to find the basket is empty. As you pulled the bucket up, you notice that the water is slowly spilling over the edge. You brought the basket up to quickly and carelessly. It is the same when you do not manage your money wisely. Think things through and understand your spending habits. Be wise with the way you use your money.

Being good with money is not only about making ends meet; instead, it makes life easier if you know how to handle your finances. You will not find yourself taking those steps backward. You know how to manage your expenses better. You are going to have the funds to pay for your obligations timely. Throughout the years, I have learned some valuable factors in saving money and planning.

Have a Budget: Budgeting is the key to financial independence. Some people think of budgeting as one way of being poor. Others will think of this as a hefty and tiresome process of creating a list of needs versus your expenses, adding numbers of monetary value, and making sure everything lines up. Yet, some think a budget will hold you back from enjoying the things you want. You only start focusing on daily needs instead of planning for your future needs.

There is a saying, *"save for rainy day."* You do not know what situation you will find yourself in. You must have savings for these unexpected issues. Budgets will allow you to prioritize your wants and needs. Despite the thoughts of those who despise budgets, you will see how this essential aspect will allow you to have more freedom to have the things you want.

Budgeting gives the order to your finances. It is creating a plan on how to spend your money. This is the layout and the blueprint to your financial freedom goal. Creating these budget plans allows you to determine in advance whether you will have enough money to do the things you want or have the things you need. It is ensuring yourself that you will always have enough money for the things that are important to you. Following a budget will keep you out of debt or take you out of obligations if you are currently in one.

Using the Budget: You have created your budget, not you must follow it. It is you executing the layout of your plan. Go over it daily and always make it a point to follow your plan as often as possible. This is you sacrificing some activities in exchange for cutting back expenses. This is you cutting your time in coffee shops and allowing you to make coffee at home. This is you eating dinner at home rather than going out to eat, and by using this budget, this is you changing your views of the value of money and focusing on what is essential.

It may sound thrifty for some, but through this, you get to understand that you only need to have the things you need to have a good life. You do not have to sacrifice a lot of money to keep up with the trends of life. Focus only on what is essential and use the budget. It will guide your spending decisions. At any given time during the month, you'll realize how much money you're able to spend and how much you have left for your savings.

Give yourself a spending limit: After subtracting your expenses and savings from your income, you can use what is left for fun and entertainment. However, you must still set boundaries. Limit yourself from spending more than you should. Before you purchase anything, make sure it will not ruin your budget.

Do not save after you spend; instead, save before you spend your earnings. Decide on a percentage of your paycheck that will go towards savings. Set this money aside, and do not touch it. This is your savings. Do this before anything else. It is the same as saying paying yourself first.

Track your spending: Refraining from online shopping is the key to success in this area. Small purchases can quickly add up. Shopping online is enticing. They draw you in to buy even if you do not need the item. Their job is to sell a product. They will use fancy words to describe and tell you why you need to buy the product. The vendors will use high-quality photos.

Before you know it, you are starting to touch your savings, and you overspent your budget. Eventually, you do not have savings. Now, if you have an emergency, where will the money come from? You need to track your spending habits to ensure you stay within your budget. One way to do this is to save your receipts and write your purchases on a spending journal.

Clean Up Your Finances
As you go along in your journey to financial freedom, you realized you'd made some financial mistakes in the past, such as wrong handling of money, overspending, and over budget. You used to focus more on treating yourself after a month of great work by buying things you thought are essential but are not. This lifestyle adds a hindrance to achieving your goal. You need to take over your finances rather than them taking over you. If you want to be financially independent, you must clean up your finances by eliminating less critical factors.

If you still have student loans, car loans, housing expenses, and debts, you must eliminate them one by one by using the Snowball Method. Focus your money on paying them off. Start making a budget by allocating your paycheck for the various loans and debts. Put your full income at their disposal. By doing so, you'll be debt-free, which is the start of gaining independence.

Paying off your debts sets the foundation for the layout of plans you create. It is building wealth that will last. Paying off debts is hard work and takes responsibility, but it is the most excellent feeling in the world with a sense of relief of keeping your money and having it at your disposal. Once your debt-free, make sure to keep it consistent; you do not want to go down that rough road again. You had debts limiting yourself in building wealth and was putting your financial plans at risk.

Be Smart About Your Career Choice
Your career puts your plan into motion. This is your biggest tool in building wealth. Make sure to think things through before deciding where you will work. Go over a list of companies, or perhaps with one's you have applied to that could provide you a comfortable workplace and satisfying income. Finding a job that supports you, especially with your goals of financial security is beneficial in keeping up with your journey.

Is there income-earning potential: Assess the company's benefits and what it has to offer. Is it beneficial to you? Is the company's salary program value you as an employee? Check the company's history with previous or active employees; this way, you will have an idea of how a company values its workers. Also, try looking for a program that can build up your finances in the coming years, such as regularization pay, salary increases, performance value, spot cash, or even converting your leave days to money. Always be on the lookout for these benefits; this could help you continue your journey in achieving financial freedom.

Can you grow: Find a company that does not only provides you with a job but also could give you a career. The difference between the two is a job that only works temporarily while a career could be a job that extends until retirement. Search for the opportunities a company can offer that could help you grow as an individual. Find a place where you can mature as this will aid you in keeping your focus in achieving your goals constant.

Do you enjoy the work: Find someplace that allows you to experience career growth and fun at the same time? Look for a working place that can enhance your passion and develop your skills. You want a company that will allow for growth.

For example, you have worked for a company for over 2 ½ years as an online teacher. They do not offer any training or room to better your teaching skills. When you come to the end of your contract, you find a company that provides training and advancement. They care about their teachers and want you to do well. This is the type of company that allows for personal growth and growth within the company.

Do the benefits support your goals of financial freedom: Look for a place you could start a career and can help you build your way to achieving your business goals. Join a company that has benefits that value you as an employee and may help you in the long run. Perhaps a company that provides a retirement plan includes health insurance or fund for emergencies as part of their employment package. Find a company that has been around for several years or decades.

Those sub-factors can help you choose an excellent place to work if you are in the market for a new job or career. You knew the different benefits that can change your perception among companies and your skills provided. Your choice of career can create an impact on your plan of achieving financial freedom; therefore, putting more focus on choosing and building your career as a priority.

Create a Strategy for Short-Term Savings

Sometimes life puts you in an unexpected situation that requires you to pull from your savings, to lend money from banks, or opening a credit card account. As we go along with life, these circumstances happen occasionally. Living from paycheck to paycheck will put you in a difficult situation. You will eventually burden yourself with debt that will consume all your income pay them off. How would you get ahead if you keep borrowing money?

If you are on a journey to gaining financial freedom, you must start owning short-term savings. You need to have a buffer for life's unexpected events. Besides having a personal savings account after paying off all your debts, you also need to create an emergency fund. These will cover all your expenses that come up unexpectedly. Having the cash on hand to cover emergencies will put your mind at ease and will not compromise your lifelong savings.

After paying off dues and creating a short-term emergency fund, you should consider preparing for big purchases that are not emergencies such as vacations. After allocating the necessary budget for every essential thing you need to save for, you can put the extra cash directly to your recreation funds. This way, when planning for a vacation, it will not be ruined with you worrying and limiting your budget.

Having financial freedom will make you prepared for every situation. Being financially independent makes you more confident in making decisions. It will give stability when it comes to finances. With a full emergency fund and a plan to cover big purchases in place, you are starting to build a life of luxury.

Learn About Your Investment Options
Investment is the allocation of your budget to an asset intended to produce an income. It could be purchased or paid through installments to acquire appreciation or generate more income higher than the amount you have invested.

After creating a short-term fund for emergency purposes, you can now turn your attention too much broader financial goals, such as investing team with a financial advisor that can help you choose the right investment decision. The advantage of this is the sooner you start spending, the longer it takes for your money to grow. Here are a few different investment options you can choose from!

Retirement Savings: Saving up for your retirement, requiring you to dispose of your income for at least 15% of your income. There are several benefits to retirement, which range from financial, personal, and psychological. Planning for retirement reduces the stress once you reached the retirement age, and all you want to do is relax. The main point was when you opted to save beforehand, and you will be able to make more efficient career-related decisions and put your focus more on your present needs and goals.

Align your retirement goals with your spouse, so you do not compromise your other financial savings goals. Make a planned budget and be consistent in following it. Planning ahead of time is significant in reaching Financial Independence. Gaining financial freedom means taking care of your future financial goals, such as your retirement.

Look for an insurance company that offers excellent retirement investment plans and start investing as early as you can. After all, insurance companies offer a lower premium when you are younger and in good health rather than when you're near the retirement age. It is better to connect with a qualified professional to discuss your options. Always be on the lookout for companies that offer retirement plans once you reach retirement age.

College Savings: If you are married and working, you may want to start saving up for your children's college fund. College fund investments are an excellent idea as this can help them avoid student loans and prevent you from getting student debts. It will also pave a way to teach them methods of financial freedom. Since basic tuition appreciates over time, it is better to have preparation since you cannot overemphasize the value of setting aside money for your children's education early on.

Real Estate Investments: Getting rid of mortgage debt can become a milestone in your journey to financial independence. Paying off your house should be a part of your plan, not something that hinders you and your goals. You must think things through on what kind of a home you will purchase and how you choose to finance it. Buying a home is a good investment. Real estate value does not depreciate over time, but it does increase its worth throughout the years.

Real Estate investment is one of the most popular profitable investments with a lot of earning potential. After paying off your mortgage, start investing by buying properties and have it rented out. Your rental features will work for you without you putting too much effort into it. Real Estate Investing will be a great source of cash. Over time, it will build your wealth.

Invest No Matter What the Market is Doing: There is no better time to start investing than now. As soon as you have the income, you might want to touch your toes into the deep waters of investing. You will be surprised how easy it is to grasp the workings of investing. Plan to invest no matter what the market is doing.

Diversify Your Investments: A diversified investment constitutes of various assets that earn the highest return or money with a small amount of risk. For instance, investing in stocks and bonds with the willingness to take risks, can signify the positive effects that you could achieve. Diversification works because these investments come from different areas.

Be Active in Your Journey to Financial Independence

Be active, which means take part in every step of your financial journey. Make it a habit to be consistent and check yourself to ensure you are tackling each goal. Be confident in making decisions such as investments or savings funds. You have already worked hard to lay the right foundation of your plan, so there is no option for you to stop. Navigate your options and make your way through it; you'll be surprised that almost all of your actions reflect your financial goals.

Create ways that could help you check your goals one by one. Here are some ways you can try!

- Find an investment professional that could provide you with the right options and could help make the right investment decisions.
- Rebalance your funds regularly to reduce risk.

- Create a realistic plan based on your capacity and limitations.
- Set up a withdrawal plan for every specific event.

It is always useful to have a plan before entering this journey. It is better you are prepared and have enough information on what needs to be done or if you are on the right track.

Decide How Bad You Want It and Do Not Be You Are Afraid

Some people are afraid of venturing out into this journey, as it takes a lot of changes to be triumphant. It also takes a long time, and hard enough to keep your drive of being consistent.

If you are new to this journey, always remember that success does not happen overnight. It takes a lot of time to build a habit and another long process in turning it into practice. For the most part, handling money is always about your expression. Yet, you do not need to go from zero to sixty overnight. Small wins are better and small steps are big one's leaps. Perhaps you can start by picking reasonable and achievable goals.

For example, if you are new to savings, then start with a small amount. Eventually, you will begin to build your savings. Starting slow will help you make the confidence you need.

Decide for yourself that these goals are personal, and abandoning this process is risking everything you have. To become financially independent, you have to be dangerous in every decision you make.

Start Creating a Series of Steps Will Help Get You Your Desired Goals
Creating a series of sub-goals are beneficial in achieving small wins. Becoming financially independent is not a single goal because financial life is composed of several factors. To reach your main objective of Financial Independence, you need to put up goals for you to achieve in certain areas of your journey.

- You are finding ways to increase your income, such as having a side job or engaging in entrepreneurship.
- They are controlling your spending habits.
- You are paying off your debts, such as student loans, mortgage, etc.
- Learn and understand your spending patterns.
- Establish investment objectives.
- Create a long-term financial goal.
- Indulge in investment plans and insurance.
- Set aside short-term funds for emergencies or special occasions.

You must start by creating a list of goals, categorize them in detail, and correspond specific steps to achieve each goal. This will ensure you are moving your entire financial situation on the right path and align your goals to your capacity. Limitations for this journey require a significant change in yourself and behavior. Success does not happen overnight. It is a long process and takes work. Have a clearer picture of your end goal, and you'll be motivated enough to push through success.

Delayed Gratification
Delayed Gratification is a term that means being willing to sacrifice your present desire and happiness for hope in obtaining a more-valued reward in the future and sacrificing for the betterment of your life and your family in the future. It gives you a chance to think about it several times if this is a want or need. If it is a need, how much of a need is it and what will it do for you and your family. It could be a spur of the moment type of buy.

In a financial term, this is the ability to wait to buy something after saving up for it, rather than purchasing it impulsively. Do you really need it now? Can you wait to buy a new one? This is one of the most significant factors for creating wealth.

Those who accumulate wealth tend to live frugal and thrifty. This is a challenging concept to learn, but well worth it. It does not necessarily mean putting off the things that make you happy; instead, merely delaying your wants. Putting off something you wish would come true, hoping for something bigger and better later. This is the key to financial success.

Cutting back expenses to make way for your necessary needs is one of the means of gratification. Here are some ideas on how you can practice delayed gratification:

- Choose to invest your money before spending it.
- Cook at home instead of eating out.
- Exercise at home or outdoors such as jogging, walking in the park, swimming, etc. instead of paying the gym's membership.
- Get a good night's sleep instead of going out on the town bar hopping and drinking.
- Stop the urge to have snacks and healthy foods.

There are a lot of ways to practice delayed gratification. It takes discipline and self-control to make it work. Focus on your goals and remember, financial success always starts with try.

Block Out the Spendthrifts in Your Life

A spend thrifty person is someone who spends a lot of money in a wasteful way. Having financial goals in your life involves avoiding your peers who spend money extravagantly on things they do not need. One of the sacrifices you may need for reaching financial freedom is either reduce your contact with types of people or letting them go. This is a necessary step to help control your urges to spend money. The people you spend time with will have a profound effect on your spending habits.

The type of people you are with can make or break your financial goals. If people surround you and have a mentality of *"live for the moment,"* they would rather spend their money and have fun instead of saving for the future; you will eventually be like them and ruining your chances of success. Nonetheless, if people with the same goals surround you, then you will have a big chance of saving big.

Always Keep Your Career or Business Moving Forward

Keep your source of income steady, and it is your career or your business as this will provides the oil in your engine. If you can steadily increase your revenue while putting your spending at a minimum, you will reach all your financial goals much more quickly.

Keep your career moving forward by keeping your work skills enhanced and sharp. This will increase your value to your employer and give you a chance for promotion. Giving yourself a better financial opportunity can help you grow your funds for your savings. If you are self-employed, keep your projects coming and invest in yourself, because it is a good return of investment.

Always Make a Commitment to Save Money Regardless of Your Income

The best time to start saving money is now, not tomorrow or not later. Do not be one of those people with the mentality of *"I will start saving money when..."* You should still be saving whenever and wherever. This is one of the best strategies to make sure you are always moving forward.

The goal of this journey is to save enough money to have a comfortable future. Always keep a record of your finances, create a budget, and go with your list daily. This will keep you on track to reach your financial goals. Determine where and when you can save big, indulge in every income opportunity, and always follow what you have planned. Start getting in the habit of saving money. You can start with a small amount, and eventually, you will reach your goals. You will be surprised how easy it can be.

Never let anything hinder you from saving money. Starting today, you are working towards the long-term goals that you created. Stop procrastinating and start saving. Try dipping your toes in different industries such as investing in stocks, real estate, bonds, etc.

Diversify Your Income Sources Too!
It is essential to have a well-diversified investment portfolio since we can never be sure what the market will do at any given time. You should never put all your eggs in one basket. If you are already investing, the best way to protect your assets is to diversify across several different classes. This will help you accumulate more wealth every time the market rises.

Always remember that a variety of investment will yield a higher return. By taking a disciplined approach and practicing diversification, you may find investing rewarding in the worst of times.

Commit to Refocusing Your Goals Regularly

Everybody wants financial independence, but not everyone will achieve it. Economic freedom is a process. It requires commitment and self-discipline for an extended period. Make a written plan that includes goals for each financial category and review them often. Have two goals in mind:

- Make sure your goals are on track.
- To keep yourself focused on your goal of financial independence.

This is very important, particularly on your second goal. It is effortless to be distracted. Perhaps, you find it surprising how much you have already spent that you call for a celebration by expenditure again. This will put you back to square one. Self-disciplined is essential in this area. Becoming financially independent is not easy. Therefore, you need a detailed plan and a commitment to continue it long-term. Use your method as a guide and modify it in your circumstances. You must never give up, no matter what life throughs your way.

Chapter 3: Getting Rich and Building Your Wealth

Everyone dreams of getting rich. You want to build your wealth, retire to someplace lovely like the Philippines, and enjoy your life. We have been talking about a lot of different ways to make your wealth, and I will break it down even further to help you get to where you want to be.

How to Get Rich: Bold Moves that will Guarantee Wealth

Most people wanted to live in financial comfort and stability. Who does not want to be well off anyway? Almost everyone wanted to be wealthy, to buy everything they want, and have access to a luxurious lifestyle. However, what does it take to become rich? While the end goal is clear; the process and where to begin seems to be the problem.

There are a few ways on where and how to get started. You must first begin to acknowledge that becoming rich will take time and effort. Almost everyone tries to be productive, yet not all of them succeed. Others were born with a silver spoon in the mouth. Some become rich through winning the lottery, yet others become successful due to their hard work and determination. Overall, the most valued trait in getting wealthy is to live SMART as the pay is great to be smart! Your income will not hold you where your mind wants to go. You must know the difference between working hard over working smart. Learn some ways on how to keep your life afloat without sacrificing anything or better yet learn how to strategize by using your resources to create more income.

Overall, being wealthy does not usually guarantee how much a person will have. Experiencing real richness comes from a place of abundance and to be fully content on what you have. However, it would be better for everyone at one point if they experience an abundance of wealth.

Start your own business: Most rich people engage in trade for easy money that comes from it. A lot of wealthy individuals are entrepreneurs, as there is only a limited amount of jobs that can make you productive.

When I started to see how easy it was to get out of debt, I wanted to educate others. I started my own business and began to build my company. I had to learn the hard way that my business could only reach the level of success based on my imagination. It is our thoughts and desires that allow us to succeed or fail.

Capitalism, or owning equity of a successful business, drives most people to succeed. This can be a significant step in making money, especially if you have a knack on selling or marketing. Create a business in your liking or based on what is trending. Gain enough knowledge to create something profitable and use your resources, such as your environment and technology to keep your business from growing. Surround yourself with people who have the same goals as you. This may seem hard when you first try but keep in mind that nothing is comfortable in the beginning. Many businessmen will tell you were creating your own business requires a massive change in lifestyle. You need to change your behavior upon reaching your goals; also, you need to become frugal at one point. You have to know the value of money more than anybody.

However, the problem with growing your own business is the imagination and desire of the individual. Most companies will fail in the first five years. Only half of these companies are driven and make a decent living from their business. Some of them did not even make it. One of the ways to reach your goal is to think smart, keep your business thriving in the market, and operate big and profitable. With determination and excellent strategy skills, you will pull through.

Join a fast-growing company: Another way to become wealthy is to join a fast-growing company. Not all people get to become rich by being employed, but as part of your *"working smart"* strategy, this could be a way for you to become one. Higher your ambition and for the best position with the most fabulous salary. Look for a fast-growing company and become either the fit or best asset this company will have.

- Enhance your skillset and values to become an asset.
- Improve your skills and learn how to use them to be on the company's right side.

- Get educated and learn your industry well.
- Position yourself strategically in the right company.

There are many ways on how you can get involved, but you must remember that there will always be a trade-off to every right side. It will take a lot of time to start and a massive amount of motivation to keep pushing yourself higher from where you are. Nevertheless, choose to be positive anyway and keep on moving forward.

Become a specialist: If you become a specialist, chances are you possess a rare, highly valuable skills. There are a variety of specialists in every field and industry; there are doctors, IT scientists, salespeople, and so on. Use this to your advantage. Your chances of accumulating wealth are higher, for the rate of failure is lower.

To be one, you need to get a formal education. These types of people get to be paid exceptionally well. They are usually *"the star"* of their job and often the most in-demand. This is due to the vast array of experiences. They typically excel in their line of work; hence they get paid more.

If you choose to be a specialist for you to get rich, you have to excel in everything you do and become the *"star"* in your field. You must become a unique value to the market by putting yourself more out there. Usually, the money circle is in your hands if you do something valuable to other people.

Secure a management position in a big or highly profitable company: In a workforce setting, the one who is usually on top of the employee chart will be the one who gets paid more. Managers are often productive for their tasks do not seem to be easy. Those managers who are employed in a big and profitable company are usually well paid.

However, some of the trade-offs of being a manager are: first, sometimes it takes too long for an employee to be promoted. It could take several years and a lot of experience before securing a good management position. Second, your competition will be hard, the further up you are in the ranks, the more politics you must deal with. These are some of the many stumbling blocks you might encounter if you consider being a manager on the road to you becoming wealthy. Yet, some made it enough to testify that this strategy works.

The frugal and slow way to wealth: Being frugal does not necessarily mean becoming poor. A frugal lifestyle is spending your money only for your basic needs and keeping the rest for your savings.

When I became debt-free, I lived a simple lifestyle and did not spend much. I started to think several times over every purchase. I would weigh my wants and needs. I would ask myself if I really needed it. Then I would go for about a week longer without it. This was a test to see how many times I did an activity that the item be beneficial for. If I did not see any benefit in buying the product, I did not. If I could see that my want was becoming a need, then I would buy it.

Get into the financial industry or become an investor: Learn the value of an investment and the magic of interest. Start while you are still and gain your money back twice the amount you have invested. If you do not have experience in investing, try hiring an agent, and learn the basics of investing. Learn the market and be on the lookout for the best investment asset to put your money on.

Start with real estate trading: Real Estate is a powerful wealth tool. A significant number of millionaires have proven it. Almost all wealthy people had at least a couple of real estate investments. Subsequently, property investment does not depreciate on value but somewhat increases in terms of pricing. In addition to this, "forced appreciation" comes to the picture. This is the concept of expanding the property's value by physically renovating the place.

There can be a lot of ways to make real investment as your source of wealth. First, after buying land, turn it into rental properties and accumulate income monthly or yearly. Also, convert it to commercial property and have it rented out to people who want to start a business. Lastly, turn your eye into buying a dilapidated house and flip it into something that can be a rental and making it livable, which you can capitalize on a wealth generator or sell it with added forced appreciation value. There is more! Here are a few ways you could speed this up:

- **Get a better deal:** Negotiate your way into a better contract. This will supercharge your growth. For example, bargain a duplex for only $200,000 instead of $250,000. Keep your eye on the market and be vigilant with these types of deals, for they do not last long!
- **Buy more deals**: The more properties you buy, the more money you can earn! Think about it! Have the cash flow running from buying properties and turn them into rental or commercial properties.
  - **Forced appreciation:** Flip houses and sell them for a much higher price.
  - **Trade up:** Have your properties bought by developers, such as a hotel or condo apartments, to maximize your return.
- **Hire a real estate agent:** These people are equipped with real estate knowledge, and they know how to turn your investment into higher returns.

There are so many different paths and strategies you could take to become wealthy through real estate. Learn from your mistakes and successes, and use it to your advantage. That is the beauty of the real estate, and all you have to do is to get involved.

Get famous: his is the most common way of becoming rich. Since attention is a valuable thing today, getting famous can help grow a millionaire. Given how technology is becoming mainstream, social media is now a platform for earning money. For example, you can make money with *"YouTube"* through the numbers of views and subscribers.

If you become a professional YouTuber, your chances of becoming rich are high. A lot of famous stars, celebrities, YouTube actors, or social media influencers make their money out of publicity. Social media builds too many high-profile people in time with unattainable lifestyles, a significant amount of properties, and too much cash in the bank. This is how certain easy fame can make you famous.

Be aware of the dangers fame can bring. Not all famous people live a great life, as a trade-off, a lot of them cannot do things that the average person can, or they always carry the worry for their own safety and the safety of their loved ones. All in all, fame is an excellent money-making career but not an easy thing to live.

Count on your luck: Finally, on your quest to find ways on how to become rich, why not try counting on your success. This is not a positive way, but it sure does not hurt trying. Make your way in playing the lottery or have a run-in with the casino's slot machines, try gambling a little, play bets in sports, etc. These are some ways to do it. There may be a higher chance of your luck, depending on how lucky you are.

These are only options, and you must still keep in mind that *"too much brings bad luck."* These options are not necessarily fit to be an effective way of becoming rich; therefore, practicing them too much can be lethal. You must control yourself doing these methods of earning money, for this is not an actual source of income.

Becoming wealthy is an actual job, and it requires a lot of work to succeed. It is a lifetime project that needs a lifetime knowledge and some serious effort. Sure, some people bulldoze their way to being wealthy, but some traveled a path far from others.

You do not have to toil hard to become rich; you just need to work smart. Have the right strategy, developed competencies, get a lot of formal education, start investing, self-manage your resources, and try some luck! Most importantly, do not give up. Many people have shown that it is possible.

There are not enough ways to summarize all the things that you can do to get rich. You will eventually get there once you start. Just do not get obsessed with money once you are there. Money is essential, but so is your morals and attitudes. Do not commit a mistake by exchanging money for something immoral. Your journey is not that worth it.

Chapter 4: Different Investment Strategies and Start Investing

For anyone who wants to get ahead in life, investing is a must. It is essential to understand where you should put your money and how to make it work for you. I want to begin with understanding investments.

Understanding Investment

Investment is the act of purchasing goods with the expectation of turning high-value returns over time. A replacement is the benefit of an investment. Iinvestmenting tends to have more of a risk. It will come with a higher level of the unknown. Your risk and the return go hand-in-hand when investing. The lower your risk means you should expect a lower return. If you have a higher risk, you should expect a higher return. Investing or speculation depends on three factors: the amount of risk taken, the holding period, and the source of profits.

Investing is a way to set aside money while living the hustles of life and making your money grow so you can fully reap the fruit of your labor in the future. This is one way to financial independence and giving yourself a better retirement. Understanding investment can be compared to planting a seed and wait for it to grow and then reaping the rewards of your work.

Brief History of Investing

The history of investing goes back in the time of the famous Code of Hammurabi, which was written around 1700 B.C. This code provided a framework for historical civilization and laws. This framework of investment, wherein debtors and creditors pledged each other's lands through collateral.

During the medieval Islamic world, the *"quad"* had been a significant financial instrument, which later became the inspiration of *"command"* used in Western Europe.

Back to the period of the 17th and 18th centuries, the Amsterdam Stock Exchange was established in 1787, followed by the New York Stock Exchange in the year 1792. During the 1800's most of the established banks, such as Goldman Sachs and J.P Morgan. In the early 1900s, purchasers of stocks, bonds, etc. have been called speculators. Then there was the crash of Wall Street in 1929.

We entered the 20th century, and it started to pave the road towards new theories in investing. The development of several new concepts was discovered, such as having asset pricing, methods in the perfect portfolio, and several different financial terms.

Types of Investments

There are so many ways to invest your money. These are just a few of the common types of investments.

Stocks: These are also called equity or capital stock. This is something that represents ownership of a portion of a corporation wherein the property is divided. Stocks give you a small purchase of a corporation in proportion to the total number of shares sold. The people who buy these stocks are called *"stockholders"* or *"shareholders,"* which entitles them to the fraction of the company's earnings. Shareholders can involve themselves in the company's growth and success through appreciation in the stock price coming out from the company's profits.

Bonds: Bonds are loans to a company or government that entitles you to a fixed rate of return. It contains a lower risk than stocks and is a much safer investment. Investors lend the government money with the condition to have it repaid for a set period plus interest. On an average note, long-term government bonds can let you earn around 5% average annual returns. If you are investing in both bonds and stocks, bonds balance the risk associated with stocks investments.

Funds: Funds are the most common types of funds, such as mutual funds, exchange-traded funds, or ETFs. These types of funds are managed by investment managers. They can help investors with all kinds of options and strategies.

Investment Trust: Real Estate Investment Trust (REITs) is the most common type of Investment Trust. These will allow you to invest in commercial or residential properties and received a return from rental income.

How to Invest Money Wisely?

Do not go right into investing without having a plan. When you rush into it, there is a chance of losing your investment. You should consider these factors before you start spending your money.

Get an Emergency Fund: Nobody wants an emergency, but it is always helpful to be prepared. An emergency fund is a fund set aside for unexpected expenses such as unforeseen medical expenses, unemployment, and repairs. Having an emergency fund creates a financial buffer that will keep you afloat without having to worry about incurring debts or borrowing money. It's always a great idea to come prepared.

Save as much as half a year of expenses. You may want to have three to six months to cover you in the event of an unexpected financial blow and prevents you from going to debt. Put it in a savings account with a high-interest rate and easy access, but keep in mind to have it separated from your regular savings to keep yourself from spending it. Having something reserved creates a difference between short-term financial critical stage and burying yourself in debts.

Pay High- Interest Debt: Saving money can be associated with paying off debts. Getting out of debt should be a top priority when saving. If you have obligations, the incurs much higher interest rate than your investment's return, and then you are most likely losing money instead of gaining it.

Paying your debts off is the best option to burden yourself, like credit cards. The amount you manage to save will not be enough to offset liabilities, especially with a compound interest rate in play. Think about the interest you are paying each month versus the amount you will likely save if you manage to avoid debts.

Aside from the financial burden of having debts, it can also have an impact on your psychological and emotional well-being. Most often, an average person with obligations will worry for at least half of their life. So, it is better to come prepared, and after creating an emergency fund, you will want to start paying off debts. As you progress through this process, you could feel a sense of security. The more active you are, the higher this feeling.

Age: Your age is one of the most significant factors you should consider when investing. How you invest can depend a lot on your age since your portfolio tells more about where you are now in life. The best way to gain more returns is to start investing once you already have the financial means. Start investing as soon as you can, and you'll be surprised to see the magic power of compound interest. When do you think the best age is to begin investing in your future?

The younger you are when you begin investing, the more time you have for your initial investments to grow, which will increase your chances to accumulate significant wealth. If you are in your 30's, you still have at least 30 years or more before you retire. You may be putting yourself in more risk, but with your age given, you will no doubt get back up because you have years to recoup your losses. You can afford to gamble during this age, therefore being aggressive in this period is likely to be helpful.

If you're closer to retirement age, you will want to cut off more expenses and to save more money. Being closer to retirement is the time to examine your future goals and keep steady your investment to provide yourself a better retirement. As you are walking your way to departure, dial back your stocks and bonds, while balancing the increase and the allocation of your investments. You might also want to assess your finances before continuing to lower the odds of risk you will be getting.

Compound Interest: This is the money you will get as a return in exchange for the amount of principal you have invested. It is the interest you earn as the interest to the principal sum or a loan deposit. Compound interest coined as *"interest on interest,"* which calculated from the initial principal and included all the accumulated interest from previous investments. Through this, you will likely earn money sooner when you start investing.

For example, you are 25 years old and just started to invest. You can save $5,000 a year. You should make it a point to keep this as a steady gain for the next 40 years. Once you reach 65 years old, you will likely have $200,000. If you invest this money with a 7% annual return, you will have made at least 1 million dollars. Thus, increasing your monthly contributions also increases the amount you will be getting, and it is even before retirement. Thanks to the power of compound interest!

It is crucial to keep in mind that investing will always be associated with risk. Thus, it will be helpful if you make sure only to spend your spare money. Investment Is a one-way source for your payment, but this should not be your primary source of income. The stock market can be fragile from day-to-day, but you are more likely to make more money in the long run if you start investing rather than not doing anything at all.

Understand Which Type of Investor You Are: When working with a financial advisor, they usually first ask, *"what are your goals and how much are you willing to invest?"* or, *"are you a risk-taker?"* These questions will identify what type of investor you are; this way, your financial advisor will provide you a better investment plan with the hopes of growing your money in the future.

DIY Investing: DIY or *"Do It Yourself"* investing requires a more hands-on approach. You will need to do all the research. Also, you need to keep track of your stocks regularly, which can be time-consuming. Yet this type of investing means you have total control of your portfolio.

Passive Investing: Some people have not woken up yet from the mindset of spending more because their lifestyle is more important than financial security. Some people are passive investors who can move beyond financial independence. Which one are you?

Passive investing is the most common form of financing. This is where the retail world of investing lives. They typically invest in all the basics of personal financial planning, such as owning a home, setting up a retirement plan, asset allocation, and disposing of their income for at least 15% towards their savings account. This strategy is suitable for people whose lives are full of matters concerning their families, jobs, outside interest, or people building businesses. Thus, it makes it difficult for them to make investing a top priority.

This is a *"set-it-and-forget-it"* approach to investing. This method of financing is for people with busy lives and opt-out to employ someone to spend for them. If this is the type of investor you are, then you can invest in mutual funds or exchange-traded funds through a Robo advisor. This platform does all the work for you, and all you need to do is set-up your investing goals with them to get started.

Investing Through Your Employer: Investing in your employer is a great business opportunity. Make use of an employer's employment contract that helps you saving money a whole lot easier. Occasions such as early retirement plan funding, some companies offer salary deduction fifty-fifty for employees who want to save up for their retirement while actively working in the company. Some companies, especially those who focus on sales, often create events that involve spot cash. This works through reaching a specific quota in exchange for a monetary amount. This will build the relationships you have with the person you work for and provide you with several sources to help you make your savings!

Invest According to Your Risk Tolerance: Since the investment market can be on and off, you need to understand how much risk you are willing to take in exchange for a higher return of money. Your risk tolerance is determined by a combination of factors, such as your investment goals, experience, the time you are willing to Putin, your other financial income, and your *"fear factor."* There may be a lot of investment options, but depending on your risk tolerance and how you are willing to lose your money for a higher return, this will decide your fate in investing. The riskier the investment is, the higher the returns.

The best thing to do is invest in a variety of different asset classes: An *"asset of classes"* is an investment with similar characteristics and subject to the same rules and regulations. They behave similarly to one another in the marketplace. Investing in one or many asset classes is also the right type of investment. This promotes diversification, which gives you a well-rounded portfolio that can carry you up within the waves of the stock market. An example of these is; investing in a mutual fund, owning different stocks across several sectors, or renting out a few real estate properties.

The Primary Asset Classes You Choose are Based on the Risk

There are several classes of assets. I am only going to mention the most common of them; however, you should research and find all your options.

Cash: Cash will also include cash equivalents. This is considered the safest investment for its value and is always steady, even when you are considering inflation. Investing in an interest-paying savings account is an easy way to expand your cash reserves.

Bonds: Bonds are known as fixed income. This is also the money you lend to a government or institution which is paid with interest in return. Examples include mutual bonds and certificates of deposit.

Real Estate: Having real estate is owning a physical property, which is also an investment. You can engage in owning a portion of property or investing in a Real Estate Investing Trust (REIT). Buying and owning real estate is an investment strategy that can be both satisfying and profitable.

Stocks: Stocks are also known as equities or profit-sharing in a company's investment. These are the most common investment strategy. However, keep in mind that the risk associated with investing in stocks depends on the performance of the company. Younger companies might be riskier, but a long-running and established company is a better idea; yet, they can go bankrupt due to unexpected changes or a lawsuit. Therefore, you should be prepared for every situation in your investments.

Futures and Other Derivatives: These are also called future contracts. This is when you focus on the future price of an underlying asset. These are the financial contracts that you can oblige to transact an asset at a given future date and price. This method is when the buyer purchases an asset from a seller with a set amount regardless of the current market price of the expiration date. There are many types of futures contracts available for trading, including:

- There commodity futures such as crude oil, natural gas, and other agricultural products.
- Consider currencies such as those in euros and the British pound.
- Do not forget the metals like figures in gold and silver.
- Finally, consider the government treasury futures and other products.

Commodities and Precious Metals: these are owning material things that can be in the form of gold, oil, or vehicles. These possessions can be traded into other things with the same value. Investing in gold or other precious metals is seen as a hedge against inflation. Most ordinary people are investing in gold, such as given its real value since it can be carried easily, worn comfortably, and do not depreciate. In general, gold is seen as a diversified investment since it can add a diversifying component in your portfolio.

Other Alternatives Investments: When building your investment portfolio, you may want to consider different alternative investment strategies. Investing in material things with great value will also bring higher returns. There are some alternatives in the financing, such as the ability to invest in some real assets. These assets could be physical or tangible and have a higher monetary value. These may include but not limited to, real estate, oil, precious metals, and agricultural land. Luxury and collectible goods will also fall under this category. They include wine, art, rare coins, or even baseball cards.

These valuable things can be an excellent addition to your portfolio. However, since they are still an investment, they will also carry their own set of risks for you to consider.

Set a Deadline and Choose an Investing Goal

Goals and investments should be hand and hand. You should create a plan that can help make the most of your money in the years to come. By now, you already figured out which investment strategy you will like the best. You currently have a better idea of the type of asset of classes you can invest then it is about time to move forward in your goals of having financial freedom.

Investing Goals You Should Consider

In everything you do, it is essential to consider your options and goals. These goals will determine the future. It helps us keep on track and continue to see our vision.

Short Term Investing: These are investments that mature to cash within a year. This strategy is best when you need the money within a year. When you opt for this strategy, you usually invest in short-term stocks and bonds and expect these assets to be cashed in quickly. These assets are called *"liquid"* if you can readily access it. Short-term investing has its pros and cons.

- **Pros of Short-Term Savings**
    - *High liquidity* provides convenience since your money is not stuck in an account for a set amount of time you will be able to withdraw your funds once you need them.
    - They are *Low risk* since it does not stay on the market for too long, making it have a small chance for an investor to take. It has less time to be impacted by the fluctuation of the market.
- **Cons of Short-Term Savings**
    - *Low return* because you had your funds invested for only a short period, and you will likely have a low yield of an investment.
    - You will have a *Higher Tax Bill* in a short period. You are still intended to pay taxes

but much higher if you leave it as a longer-term account.

Long-term investing: These are investments in a company that intends to hold for more than a year. The difference of this from the short-term investment is long-term investments are not likely to be sold for only a year, and in some ways, they may never be sold. With this strategy, your account appears on the asset side, in which other investors are willing to take on more risk for higher returns.

- **Pros of Long-Term Investing**
    o *Less risky* the longer you have invested. There is a higher chance you can recover from an investment downfall.
    o *Less Stressful* as you do not need to follow markets regularly.
- **Cons of Long-Term Investing**
    o *You need patience,* as this is a long-term investment. Since this is a part of your financial freedom goal, patience is considering important.
    o *Less Control* the longer you invest, the more time you're your investment in the market, allowing for an extended return of your money.

Define your Investment Budget

Having a budget helps save money for you to use in investing. Make sure to include plenty of funds when investing. Since the market is unpredictable, investments are one way to increase your source of income. Investing should never be your top priority in looking for money. You must still obtain a job and engage in other sources of financial activities.

Defining your budget first before risking it into investments is one of the first steps you should consider. How much money are you willing to gamble? How much money should you start with? These are only a few questions you should ask yourself before entering the world of investing. Better yet, hire a financial advisor who could help determine the right choices to make. Ask for a consult on what investment strategy will be best and how much should you need to dispose of to get ahead and be prepared for the future.

Investing paves the way to attain financial independence. You simply need to try and make the decision to keep it longer until you receive favorable outcomes. There is no perfect plan to save money, only the determination and persistence for you to keep moving forward. You need to remember that prudent investing is not just about what you invest in but also about how you spend. It is not impossible to invest if you only a small amount of money.

To make the most of your investment and gain a higher return, you must educate yourself on the basics of how to make a stock investment. You must be confident and familiar with yourself using all the resources that you can get. Make use of the internet, peers who are already investing, financial advisors, or even attending seminars. These resources are available to help you evaluate stocks and find ways to protect the money you will earn. Every investment comes with risks.

The higher the return comes with higher risk and vice versa. Therefore, you must learn how to be confident and make sure to have a separate savings plan and an emergency savings fund to keep yourself afloat even when the stock or investment market is down.

Investment Strategies

For a lot of people, the most common way of making money is to get paid based on the number of hours you work. Entering the workforce is a good source of income; however, this strategy is limited, which makes it impossible to get rich. Check your income based on the number of hours you worked, minus your expenses and necessities. How much remains? You probably have less than 15% of your income to put off as savings. The desirable savings amount should be no less than 15% of your income.

The probability of you earning a million dollars is having to work a lifetime without wasting a single dollar, which makes it unreal. Also, by the time you have set the amount you wanted to save for as the value of money to be less, which will bring you back to work again.

Think about it, what if I told you there could be another way round? Somehow, you have savings, but you have no means to put it to work. You thought, putting it in a savings account is probably the best idea you have done. Well, think again. Maybe, now is the best time to think about investing. I am sure you thought of investing before, but you never did it. Perhaps it was because you never understood it. Investing is complicated, but not as much as you think it is. The best thing about investing is putting your money to work for you.

You will see fun it is to Make the value of your money worth twice as much. Investing is not only for people with money; the best way for you to find out how it works is to start learning about it. How much money it requires, and how can you make it work? Learning the basics of investment will take you on your journey of financial freedom.

Every savings investor needs to know the difference between saving, investing, and speculating. These three terms will help you understand the world of investments, which will lower your risk of losing a lot of money.

Saving is a process of setting money aside to purchase for a shorter period, perhaps under three years. The importance of savings is securing the safety of your money, thus putting it in a bank is a good idea; unfortunately, as a trade-off for protecting your money, a savings account will pay a low interest and creating a continued growth of your investment.

If you want to earn more than what you can save, you must look at investing. This is a long-term process that involves committing some of your money to own a portion of a company's shares. There are many ways to invest with stocks, bonds, and real estate as the most popular types of investment. Yet, as a trade-off, investing carries more risk due to the value of your investment is unpredictable. To be a successful investor, you must invest your money in the market for at least three years for your investment to appreciate enough to give you a higher return.

You are speculating, the need to grow your money quickly. It involves putting your money at risk with the expectation that you will get a higher return in a short period. The road to financial freedom is not simple, and you need to work hard and make yourself more disciplined than you were before. It pays to be wise. Knowing the difference of each way you can save money will pave your way to success. There are no shortcuts in this endeavor, but there are better ways of how to make more money; you only need to be smart.

How to Choose an Investment Strategy: Investment strategies are flexible. You can choose a variety of techniques that could work for you the best, or you can make changes to satisfy your goals. Investing requires you to have a more significant amount of funds to get started. Since the market is unpredictable, it can be expensive at first. Every purchase carries a fee, and gaining a high return is taxable.

Here we look at strategies that will help suit your financial goals. By taking the time to understand the characteristics of each one, you will be putting yourself in a better position to choose one that is right for you and can work for in the long run.

Take some notes: Researching before beginning to dip your toes into the water of investment is helpful. It is essential to gather the necessary information that can help you determine how you reach your goals. You need to analyze your financial situation first. Align your income to the amount you are willing to invest in. Here are some take-away questions that you can ask yourself when investing:

- What is your current financial situation?
- How much is your cost of living, including monthly bills and debts to pay?
- How much can you invest?
- How much risk are you willing to take?

Not owning a lot of money should not be a hindrance for you to be successful. The only way to make this possible is for you to start investing. First, you need to pay off your debts then consider creating a separate savings account before you start putting money aside for investment.

Next, plan your goals and determine your financial needs. Do you want to save up for retirement? Are you looking to purchase something big? Perhaps a new house or a car in the future? Or are you saving up money for your children's college fund? Establishing your answers to these questions will help you create an investment plan that could put you in a stable financial situation. Figuring out your tolerance for risk is crucial.

Strategy 1: Value Investing
This strategy focuses on purchasing undervalued stocks from big companies for a more extended period. Undervalue stocks do not fully reflect the natural value of the security of the company. Value investing is intelligent investing. You are focusing on spending on companies you think are undervalued hence making them good quality companies. Investors make their decision based on stable fundamental analysis. They trust their intuition more than anything, yet they are still completing an in-depth analysis before investing, thus making them intelligent investors.

Value Investing Tools: The price-earnings ratio (P/E) has become the primary tool for quickly identifying underrated stocks or cheap stocks. This way, you do not have to perform an in-depth analysis or thorough research. Using the P/E method, you measure the company's current share price relatives to its per-share earnings (EPS). This is called the price multiple or earnings multiple.

This shows that a lower P/E ratio signifies you are paying less per $1 of current earnings. The lower P/E ratio signifies an excellent company performance, and a high rate means the company stock is overvalued. Most investors are looking for companies with a lower P/E ratio.

The critical thing to remember is there are no set of rules you can apply in investing. You must be keen on what is going on in the world since the market mostly relies on world events and every country's economy. If the economy is experiencing trouble or in a global health crisis, then corporate earnings can be affected or become lower. On the other hand, during booming economies, revenues go up and continue to rise.

Strategy 2: Growth Investing

Growth investors want investments that offer substantial deals when it comes to earning higher returns. Growth as an investment strategy focuses on increasing the investor's capital in which you, as the investor, invest in stocks that are growing. This is a strategy that focuses on businesses. It has a more significant potential for growth within the industry. Investors believe in the value of the company, thus making the value of shares and their purchase rise. They seek out to be the pioneer of their products and want them to become a leader in a specific and promising industry. There are two sub-strategies associated with growth investing:

- **Short Term Investments** are when investors buy stocks for less than a year. Most often, they used this strategy when they think a company's value is likely to go up quickly.
- **Long-term investments** are held for more than a year. This strategy is used by investors as they believed the company's value would grow slowly and steadily over the years.

These companies often offer a few benefits for investors.

An ample and expanding market opportunity: Growth stocks produce revenue growth of 10% per year or more over an extended time. They become the leader in a specific chance of a promising industry and then expanding its market. Then, these new markets let the company grow revenue as it gets more prominent in the future.

A durable competitive advantage: Growth stocks put a company in a favorable or superior business position. As a growth investor, you must look for a business with a durable competitive advantage. A business that has a network will affect what gains more customers by putting their products online, high switching cost, which turns customers to selling providers, companies who have low-cost producers, and offers intangible assets like brand awareness.

Financial resilience: This is a company that can withstand life events that impacts its income or assets. A growth investor considers every aspect of the industry in which stocks thrive. Growth stocks should be growing. As an investor, you should look for a company that has consistently strong earnings and revenue, signifying a capacity to deliver on growth expectations. You also need to understand the company's management and executive team planning actions, the previous record of history, and its recognition from the public. Recording this data can make your decision in which the company invests best.

Strategy 3: Momentum Investing

This is a system of buying stocks or other securities that have a higher return in the past year. Investors using this strategy rides the wave and looks for stock experiences for an uptrend. They believe the one who lost money will choose to short-sell those securities; however, this practice is risky.

Investors using this strategy buy stocks when they are heating up and sell them when they cool off. The concept of momentum investing is the idea of earning long term profits while riding stocks as they are on a higher return and selling them once they go down.

This is a good investment strategy; however, it can require a good deal of work. If you were to follow this method, you need to have the time, energy, or expertise to research which stocks give higher returns and those who do not. The theory of momentum investing involves following specific market indicators that tell you when to buy and sell these investments.

Strategy 4: Dollar-Cost Averaging

Dollar-cost-averaging (DCA) is a smart strategy for building investment positions over time. By doing so, you invest equal money amounts in the market at regular intervals. This is means executing whatever approach you chose for making regular investments in the market for a period without using any strategy mentioned above. You may want to create an investment account every month.

- The total sum to be invested.
- The window time you want to make the investments; daily, weekly, monthly, or any time. Think about the intervals for your investment.
- The number of times you will invest.

It is a wise choice for most investors to use this strategy. It will put your focus on saving while reducing the level of risk and the effects of vitality. This strategy is appropriate for most investors since they are not able to make a single, substantial investment. To those who are looking to invest in a lump sum, this might not be a good idea.

Strategy 5: Socially Responsible Investing
Socially Responsible Investing (SRI) enables investors to grow their money. It allows you to invest in industries or social clauses you care about. These investments bring your assets higher while making a difference.

This strategy is known as ethical or green investing, which means you only chose to spend on companies reflecting your advocacy and refraining from industries that negatively affect the environment and its people. These are companies such as those who produce or invest in alcohol, tobacco, gambling, and weapons. SRI means investing in companies that have ethical and socially conscious themes such as environmental causes or social justice.

SRI investors look for environmental, social, and corporate governance, also known as ESG criteria. These criteria alone help many socially responsible investors know which the best company is to invest as they believe these companies have the traits which can yield the most significant returns.

If this is the kind of investor you think you are, you have several options. You can invest through mutual funds, exchange-traded funds, and index funds. You must still follow the same necessary steps in spending, such as identifying your risk factor, how much are your current income, the existing investments you have, and your retirement plan. The only thing that has been added to this equation is you need to consider what a company stands for. This is in addition to what they might earn.

Strategy 6: Small-Cap Investing

The term *"small-cap"* is the capitalization of a company's market. A small-cap stock refers to those companies whose market fund ranges from $300 million to $2 billion. Investors using this strategy do not look for more prominent companies to invest in; instead, they focus on smaller companies they think will do well in the future. If you are eyeing this strategy, then you have some pros and cons to consider.

- **Pros of Small-Cap Investing**
    - Growth potential is the same as other companies. Small-cap companies show significantly higher income potential. They become attractive for other investors because they have a larger room for future

growth compare to the large-cap companies. They also grow their operational and financial base higher than large-cap companies.
- o They have a high probability of inefficiencies in the market.
- o Financial institutions do not push prices up.
- **Cons of Small-Cap Investing**
  - o High Risk
  - o Low Liquidity
  - o Time-consuming

Investing Tips

Investing is not always easy, especially when you want to have your earnings bring you maximum capacity, yet you do not know how to achieve it. That is why having a financial advisor or signing up for a Robo advisor is always a good idea. They can manage your investments according to your business goals, preferences, and, most importantly, the number of your finances. This way, you will be getting the best return for your money.

Chapter 5: Ways to Handle Your Money While Investing

There are many ways to handle your money when you invest. Some are better than others. You should choose which approach is best for you. Do you want to see your money grow? Start by finding ways to handle the money. It is essential to be organized.

Decide on How Much Help You Need

It is easy to do it yourself. Get on the internet and start researching. However, there is a much higher risk when you take matters in your own hands. You could risk losing all your investment. Can you afford to take that risk? Most of us cannot! Many people live from paycheck to paycheck and invest what little money they have. Others invest all their savings so that it will grow for retirement. The point is you do not have room to take these significant risks.

If you do not want to take the risk, try hiring someone to invest for you. Keep in mind, I would not trust just anyone with my money. Do not have your friends or family handle your investments. If they are good at investing and do it themselves, I would ask for advice. Do not let them do it for you. This is your money, and you want it handled with care. Although, I would trust a professional who does this for a living. It used to be very expensive. Today, a professional advisor can be very affordable.

Try having a robot-advisor. These are computers that have the most advanced technology and algorithms on the market. They are fully equipped to help you with your investments. They will help you build and manage your investment portfolio. The best things are through their automotive services, they can rebalance and optimize taxes. If you get into a situation to talk to someone, they can direct you to a professional where you will get to speak to an actual person.

Set Goals and Deadlines

Having a goal is essential for any investment. You should know what you are investing your money in. It does not matter if you are doing this for yourself or hiring a professional. You must have a goal and set a deadline to achieve that goal.

For example, you may have a long-term goal. These goals are usually retirement, a down payment for your dream home, or your children's college fund. These long-term goals are generally the focus of investing your money.

You may also invest in a short-term goal. These goals may be your vacation to England next year, buying a house next year, building up your emergency fund, or your Christmas gift fund for next year.

Most people who are needing money for short-term goals are day trading and not investing in the future. Remember, there is a bigger reward the longer you are invested.

Choose Your Investment Account Type

The type of investment account you choose may vary depending on your type of investments you will have. For example, your bank has different kinds of accounts such as savings, checking, certificates of deposit (CDs), and money market accounts. Each of these types of bank accounts has different interest rates. Therefore, some accounts are better than others. Although they also have their advantages and disadvantages.

The same goes for investment accounts. Several different types have their advantages and disadvantages. It is your job to do the research and decide on what type of account is best for your needs.

There are taxable and non-taxable investment accounts. If you are planning for retirement, I will use your employer's retirement plan. Many times, they will have a matching program that will help you gain better savings. Remember, if you put your money into this type of retirement, your money generally goes to the retirement account before it is taxed. That means, when you pull out the money are retirement age, all the money is subject to be taxed at that time.

There is also an option of starting your own retirement fund through a 401(K) or Roth account. This is when you use the money from your paycheck to invest in your future. That money has already been taxed. However, the interest you earn with your investment has not and is subject to be taxed. Both of these types of accounts have penalties if withdrawn early. They are designed for retirement.

If you are investing for any reason other than retirement, you may consider a taxable account. There are no tax advantages with these types of accounts, and you can withdraw the money whenever you are ready. Do your research and find out what account would be best for your needs.

Open Your Account

You have done the research. You know your options. You may have even made a list of all the pros and cons of the types of accounts you want. That is great. The water is deep, you are now ready to take baby steps and dip your toes. It is time to open your account.

You have two primary choices. You can have an online broker or go automated with a Robo-advisor. The option is yours. I already explained a little about the Robo-advisor earlier. It is completed computerized. It is like putting your investment on autopilot. If you want to be handed entirely off with your investment and trust an advanced computer to handle your money, this is the way to go. You would not need any initial deposit, and you could set up a direct transfer from your paycheck if you wanted. You will usually have an annual service fee between 0.25% and 0.50%. Keep in mind, you will not have any control over your investment.

If you want to most control over your money, try using an online broker. These brokers give you full control over buying and selling. You will also have access to investment options such as funds, bonds, stocks, and some more sophisticated investment options. This is the best option for a hands-on approach with your investment.

For those who want more hands-on, I would recommend finding a broker who has the option to practice investing using real market data. This is especially helpful for those who do not know anything about investing.

Choose Your Investment Strategy

You have everything set up. You are ready to start investing. One more thing to think about. How much risk are you willing to take? This could vary depending on your goals. For example, if you are investing in retirement at age 21, you may not need to take much risk to reach your retirement goal by 62. However, if you did not start saving for retirement until you are 45, you may want to take more significant risks for you to retire at 62. Keep in mind, the higher the risk, the greater the return.

Mutual funds, bonds, and stocks are the most known types of investments. If you want a safer investment, you may start with bonds. You typically will not lose money with bonds. However, the payout is not as big either.

For more of a risker avenue, try trading stocks. Stocks are a way for you to invest in a company. Your revenue is based on how the company did for that quarter. If they did terribly, you could lose money. If they did well, you could make a lot of money.

Mutual funds will allow you to do it all. You can invest in several different funds from bonds to stock and even other types of investments. For the best investment, you will want to diversify your portfolio. You will ant a combination of stocks and bonds. The bonds will keep money coming in, while the stocks will add some risk but could be beneficial to your investment.

For a high-risk factor, you will want more stocks and stock funds. This will bring the highest return on your money. However, it could cause you to lose a lot of money. You must have the patience to understand how the market rises and falls. Stick with it and be hands-on. If you do not like watching the market on this roller coaster, you may want to have more bonds than stocks. One thing to remember, you do not wish to play wholly safe or completely risky. Add balance to your portfolio.

Chapter 6: Best Ways to Save Money Faster in a Month

We were all kids once. We were taught the importance of money and why it is so essential to saving at a young age. We always come across the topic of financial management, even at a young age. We had school lessons about wealth, money, and tips on saving money. We were taught about how the world revolves around money; we heard bad and good stories about the consumption of the capital. Thus, the famous word coined *"money is the root of all evil"* or *"money can't buy happiness"* always made its way into our vocabulary.

Money has an essential role in our lives. Often people cannot live without money, as it is defined as the tool that enhances people's living. Money helps people to achieve a better quality of life. Accumulating wealth tells a lot of our status in life. However, the value and consumption of funds always depend on the works of men. People have high regard with wealth that most often, once they have it, spending it is still a better idea.

Saving up money should become everyone's goal. We all have goals in life. People want to achieve something, whether great or small. At some point in our lives, we thrive on accomplishing some great feats. It is part of the reason we are the way we are.

Your achievements will give you a feeling of relief. This is the same with saving, setting aside money, and accumulating your wealth; which, are all critical goals. One can never have too much until they save more than enough. Those who exercise the discipline of saving will lower the probability of entering a financial crisis.

Some people look at saving as laughable, especially the idea of saving money when you do not even have enough to get by. The reason why people laugh about saving is that they do not know where to start. Yet, you must start somewhere. If you work hard to achieve your goals, your situation will improve in time. It is worth the effort to save money and will be beneficial to you in the future.

This is a step-by-step guide for how to save money, which can help you develop realistic and straightforward strategies for you to keep all your short-term and long-term savings goals. Here are a few tips on how to save money.

Stop Relying on Willpower

Saving money is not about having the will to keep your money, but rather, it is the decision to start saving. The best time to spare is now not later. You may have several attempts in the past, yet you fail. If trying harder did not work at that time, then it probably will not work now. If you are serious about saving money, putting it off will not take you anywhere. You must have the decision to start, create a plan, put up a system that will work in all ways, and keep everything consistent.

It is not willpower that will take you to the finish line, but rather self-discipline, determination, and perseverance to help you succeed. Risk everything and do not think of quitting; you will only have the option to get back up and continue moving forward.

Be realistic

Set your goals in line with your capacities and limitations. Do not set goals that you cannot reach. Plan out carefully the things you want to achieve and map out a way that could help you reach them. If your married, create a dialogue with your partner to have a common ground on your journey to financial independence.

For instance, determine the amount of your income and how much you wanted to save, categorize each area you wanted to keep for, and allocate your budget in each area. Follow this step every day or every time you have a chance for money. This is mostly the start of financial freedom, and everything begins with the decision to try. Making gradual changes to your habits over time is one key to success.

Pay yourself first

Instead of paying off your expenses before saving what is left, why not reverse it and do the other way around? Why not start with saving up your money early before making expenses. The first guide in saving is to include your money to save in your monthly budget. Control yourself from spending unnecessary costs. Every time you receive your paycheck, you must always prioritize savings then pay your expenses using what is leftover, adjusting it as needed to make it work.

Paying yourself first is the best personal finance strategy to increase your savings and making it a consistent investment while also practicing frugality. The goal of this strategy is to make sure you keep on track with your goals saving before paying other expenses or making discretionary purchases.

Automate your savings

One of the best saving strategies for saving money is to make it automated. When you automate your savings, you are making a consistent priority to see your savings grow. Make use of the fast-growing progress of technology. Make yourself aware of the different aspects of technology that can help you with your goals. Look out for something that can provide you convenience and comfort; while helping you achieve financial freedom. There are a few essential methods that you can use to automate your savings.

Many banks will allow you to set you an automatic transfer of your money. You can set your checking account to send a set amount of money to your savings each time you get paid or on a set day.

Save money from every paycheck: This is the *"pay yourself first"* method of saving. After receiving your paycheck, save it first before spending it. One of the best ways to pay yourself first is to enroll in your company's tax-advantaged retirement plan, such as a 401(k) plan. This way you may be able to save a percentage of your salary and your employer will match the number of your contributions, up to a specific rate. Some companies will match 100%; while, other companies will not go that high. Check with your company to see what they will do to help your retirement.

Another way is to set up a checking account in a bank and start making deposits monthly. You will be likely to incur appreciated value of interest as time goes by.

Use technology saving apps: There are mobile applications that can help you make your saving routine efficient and convenient. There are a variety of apps and saving tools in the market to offer people innovative ways to save money. Be on the lookout for these types of apps, and there are sure a lot of them!

Track your savings progress: In connection with your plan on how to save money, you also need to have a progress tracker. Perhaps it can be a journal, ledger, or an excel spreadsheet that contains data such as the date, pending contributions, and savings. Every time you have your paycheck, you transfer the amount of income from pending to the savings column, then total the amount you have already saved.

There are a lot of ways on how you personalize your progress tracker. The important thing is keeping yourself updated on your advancements. Whatever updating method you will use allows you to see the results of your labor, which can be a reassuring and fulfilling experience.

When cutting expenses, think big, then small: Focus your attention on where you can save the most money for the least amount of effort. Small things such as reducing the cost of your bills, lessening your consumption of unhealthy foods are sometimes helpful. Still, the more significant impact comes from thinking of considerable ways to save money. This will help you see the fruits of your labor quickly without putting too much effort into it. Also, this can provide momentum for achieving your goal, which is essential.

When saving money, determine some factors that eat up a chunk of your budget. Think of how much money you can save when you cut them off. Start practicing replacing your other expenses for a much lower price but the same item. Nonetheless, why not figure out a way to still have this thing but in a much lesser amount.

Examples of Ways You Could Save Cash with Less Effort

Do not think it takes a lot of time to save money. It does not. In fact, it can be the most natural thing you do. Make it effortless instead of feeling like a chore.

Bring Your Lunch to Work Instead of Eating Out: Start making your meals instead of buying them, and you will be surprised how much you can save. I want you to calculate how much you spend on lunch when at work. Perhaps, you go to Burger King and get a full meal for around $7 to $10. Yes, you will get a drink, a burger, and fries. Yet, how complete will you be? I know when I go out to eat fast food, I am hunger again in 30 minutes. You go to work 5 days a week with a $10 meal from Burger King. That is $30 a week. You spend about $120 a month on food while working. When you bring your own lunch from home, you get something that will give you the energy to get through your day, and you save $120 a month.

Shop around for a cheaper cell phone plan: Keeping up with the trend of cellphone technology will likely ruin your chances of saving money. Have the mentality that you only need a mobile phone only for communication and not for modernization.

You do not need all those extra features most phone plans will give you. List down all the features your phone plan has to offer. Now go for a full month and see how many of those features you actually use. You may be surprised. The features you use on a daily bases are offered by every phone company. Why are you paying so much for a higher phone plan?

Cut unnecessary subscriptions or membership fees: These subscriptions can take away a large amount of your income. Since they occur every month and sometimes there are individual companies that increase their charges without you knowing it. These subscriptions are not being used regularly and wasting your money.

Most of these subscriptions can be used by multiple streaming devices such as Netflix, Hulu, Spotify, gym subscriptions, etc. Instead of paying it fully, why not share it with other users and have them pay for half the price. Consider sharing memberships with your family or friends. They may enjoy the benefits of these memberships and help with the costs. This way, you still get a sense of enjoyment while reducing costs.

Cancel the memberships that you do not use often and make sure to turn off the *"auto-renew"* option. The next time you subscribe to something, think of these options first. It will not hurt you; instead, it will help you save money.

Make a gradual lifestyle change: Gradually working yourself towards change will improve your odds of success. Changes may either be positive or negative, but change is necessary. Change is usually gradual, and the important thing is you put your commitment in every step.

You will learn some of the basics that you need to know on how to get started. If you are following them, then you are already on track. For instance, setting your savings automated and reducing some of your more significant monthly expenses shows that you are now paving the road to financial freedom. This keeps your progress going, and it is about time you consider making some lifestyle changes to save more money each month.

Remember delayed gratification? You might have started letting off some of the things you used to have before and started consuming only the basics. However, saving money does not entirely mean sacrificing the things you love but creating and designing a budget that matters to you. After all, one of the end goals in this journey is to bring you self-satisfaction.

Some people opt-out of the action of saving, for it takes a longer time to see its effects. For others, the work requires a drastic change in behavior, which makes it more difficult. Figure out where you can save money on things that will not affect your quality of life as much.

Examples of Some Easy Ways to Save on Your Expenses

Shop at a more budget-friendly store. This is a great way to save money. Sometimes, you can also find name brands at a discounted rate. Why buy something expensive when you can get the same thing at a better price. Here are some other ideas which will help you on your path to saving money.

- I am switching from name brand to generic prescription medications.

- Switch to outdoor training and home workouts instead of subscribing to a gym membership.
- Stop eating out and start cooking for yourself and your family at home.
- Make your coffee instead of buying coffee shops.

There are a lot more ways you can incorporate savings. Start living modestly and gradually work your way up. The critical thing about conservation is to spend less and save more. For you to save a large amount of money, you will want to follow these suggestions. Keep in mind, you have a dream and desires to change your lifestyle and way of living.

Brainstorm ways to increase your income: Think of the way wherein you can increase your revenue. Shift your mindset towards saving and cutting expenses. This will put you on the path towards saving more money each month. However, a great take away in making your journey more comfortable is looking for a few sources of **extra** income.

Be on the lookout for a few money-making activities to do during your downtime. Look for a part-time job or engage in business. There are a lot of ways that could help you advance your financial stage. You can participate in one and have it consistent.

One of your options is negotiating for a raise in your company. Improve your career performance that will put your way into a promotion. Others are participating in some transportation booking apps such as Uber or Lyft. You could try babysitting, cleaning houses, busing tables, working for a food delivery service, or countless other options. The only limitation of this list is your thoughts. If you can think of it, there is a way to make money. You are giving you a limitless amount of business opportunities.

Check your working hours if you can engage in a part-time job. Having these options will help you to build your savings and have some extra money.

Cut down on groceries: Groceries are one of the things that eat up a big chunk of your budget. Most people are often surprised to see how much they are spending at the grocery store each month. For some, buying groceries brings a relaxing feeling, yet it is so easy to walk through each aisle, grabbing a bag of Oreos here or a few bags of chips there, but those little purchases add up and end up ruining your budget.

Save money by cutting down your grocery expenses. You can start planning out meals for a week and making use of whatever is left in your pantry before heading to the store. Make a list of the things you only need to buy before getting groceries and stick to it as much as you can. Create a shopping routine and start stockpiling. Get in the habit of keeping a month of food stocked up. Re-use leftovers at home to eliminates food waste, which saves you from making another meal.

These are just some of the steps to incorporate savings in buying your groceries. They will be useful if it turns into a routine, making it a part of your daily life.

Borrow instead of buying: One of the things that adulthood brings is the accumulation of a lot of stuff such as home décor, tools that you only use once, clothing, and even seasonal decors. Over consuming is one of our traits that is unbeneficial yet inevitable. However, to avoid piling up unnecessary things, one course of action is to borrow instead of buying.

Not buying something comes with the distinct advantage of not having spent money on something you would rarely use. You do not need to purchase every tool for creating something new. Try borrowing from your family and friends, but make sure to keep them confident that you will return it as soon as you finish.

Observe two protocols in borrowing things: First, check if you keep on borrowing the same tools multiple times already, if this is the case, then it is beneficial for you to have your own.

You must be willing to lend out your tools and gear if you expect the same in return. Always keep in mind that you cannot borrow if you cannot return the same favor.

Pack lunch (and eat at home): Have you heard the phrase *"Pack your lunch; Pack your wallet?"* The cost of eating out sometimes doubles the price of packing your lunch for work or making meals at home. Think about the money you save by reducing the value of your meals instead of frequently eating out. Packing your lunch can provide you several benefits from saving money to improving your physique. For example, making your meals is knowing what you eat. By then, you can count the number of calories you consume.

The benefits are apparent when preparing lunch the night before work every day, and you will likely save time and money. With the help of preparation, you can quickly develop a system that will work well, and eventually, you will get used to it.

Try a spending freeze: A spending freeze is a period during which you somehow avoid spending. Do not buy any non-essential items for a week or even a month. A spending freeze re-evaluates your financial priorities, appreciates what you have, and boost your savings account.

Using this method does not entirely mean eliminating the action of paying your bills and buying essential groceries. Still, it places a temporary hold on things that used to be relevant to you. An example of this is making use of your pantry or filling up your tank.

This action can build your willpower, jumpstart your savings, get your budget on track, and put your focus on what is essential.

Make use of DIY's: Before you dispense a significant amount of cash for a fancy lampshade or a light fixture, think about making it yourself. You might have the skills to make one, and doing it yourself can help you save a lot of money. The cost of materials and a YouTube video can save you a ton of money rather than buying it at the store.

DIY cost less money most of the time, not only for labor cost but also for acquiring the knowledge to understand the intricate details of creating an expensive product. By doing so, it will enhance your creative skills and fun side. For example, when you are doing some home remodeling, instead of buying pillowcases at the store, why not make something. Often, people are eventually selling their DIY products in the market, making this an opportunity to bring in additional income.

Sell everything you do not need: Get rid of the things in your home that you do not use or that you are willing to let go of for the benefit of your financial future. Start selling the stuff you do not use anymore, get rid of the items that are soiled and worn. You will be surprised how much cash you can make after all this.

Selling your possessions that do not add value to your life anymore contributes to positive effects in your life. Not only you get to empty your storage room, but you also feel good about detaching from the stuff you do not need. Once you have a precise method, you will eventually get efficient and effective. Letting go of your hard-earned possession may be the most painful part of the process, but this is where you will likely make the most significant chunk of your saving. After all, it pays to sort and sell sometimes.

This reading only serves as a guide in your journey for Financial Freedom. I cannot guarantee a high rate of success. Everything else still depends on how you work for it. Your priorities and how you put value to your goals will determine the result of this process.

There is no perfect plan for savings. Sometimes the hardest thing about conservation is how to get started. It is always your determination and persistence that will keep going. No matter how error-free your plan is, if you do not have the motivation to get started and to continue, everything else will become useless.

Financial independence is not a comfortable journey, but some people make it. Therefore, the success of your trip always depends on you.

Chapter 7: Setting Up a High-Interest Bank Account for Free with No Set-up Fees

A bank account is essential when you are handling money. These accounts are significant. Today, you cannot do anything without a bank account. Businesses do not send checks in the mail anymore. The question remains, *"how can you get your bank to work for you?"* The answer is simple. Find a bank that has a high interest yet does not have any fees to set up and maintain.

Several years ago, people would go to a bank to handle all their financial needs. As things began to evolve, fewer and fewer people do bank this way. It is a digital world. Even those banks we have been accustomed to seeing, have started to convert to a digital atmosphere. They have apps and websites that will do everything you can do in the bank except take out the money itself. Traditional banking is a thing of the past.

What Are Some Benefits of Banking Online?

There are several benefits you should consider. Not every bank has the same benefits attached to their services. They are different in their own way.

Low to No Fees: The beauty of banking online is the fees. You can get much lower costs from an online bank.

However, some banks offer no prices and still have a high-interest rate for the accounts. If you are in the Military or a Veteran, you can consider USAA or BBVA. Both banks will allow you to open an account with new fees. BBVA is also open to students and not just the military. Another bank is Chime. They will cover your overdraft protection for around $100 with no added fees. This protection will include foreign and transaction fees.

Interest Rates are Better: Through an online bank, you will get a much better interest rate. Most online banks will have a 1% to 2% more interest rate than a traditional account. That is a significant difference. In conventional accounts, it may only be about 0.01% to 0.20%. Let us do the math. If you take $10,000 and invest in a traditional bank, you would only earn $1 with your savings for the entire year. That is not a very good return. Now let's look at CIT Bank. This is an online bank that offers 0.95%. Using that same $10,000, you would have earned $95 for the year. Imagine what you would make if it was at the higher end with 2.00%.

More Accessible: The traditional banks have their typical banking hours. That means you are limited on when you can check on your money and investments. The great thing about online banking is the 24/7 access. This means you connect to your bank from anywhere in the world. It does not matter what time it is.

With online banks, you have access to thousands of ATMs worldwide. For example, VARO has access to over 55,000

ATMs with no fees. These ATMs are placed in all your major stores.

Online Experience is Better: Most traditional banks have been journeying into the digital world with bill pay online and their apps. However, they do not offer the same experience as online banking. Banking online has more options and much better customer service. With an online bank, you can contact a representative at any time. That means, if you have an issue at midnight, you can call the bank and still get someone who can help.

Online Banks Have a lot to offer: You may not think so, but an online bank offers a lot of different services that many traditional banks do not. They also provide all the services that conventional banks have only with a better rate.

What to Consider and to Set Up Your Account

Do your research and find the bank that is best for you. What type of accounts do you need? Find a bank that offers everything in one location. This will make it easier to manage your money if it is all in one place. Some of the things to look for are:

- Do they have a savings account? Preferably high-interest savings account.
- Do they have a checking account? Preferably high-interest checking account.
- Do they have a Money Market Account (MMA)?

- Do they have Certificates of Deposit (CDs)?
- What are the interest rates on each of the accounts? Do your research. These will vary depending on the bank.
- Ae the insured by the FDIC? You want to make sure they are a legit bank.
- What type of ATM access do they have, and what are the fees? These will also vary depending on the bank.
- Do they have check writing and debit card access?
- Do they have investment accounts?
- What types of retirement accounts do they have?

These are only a few of the many questions you may ask about online banks while you do your research. I would suggest starting with your own list of questions based on your individual needs.

After all your research, you finally found a bank you would like to go with. Setting it up can be easy or hard. It all depends on the bank requirements and if you can get the required documents. Each bank will usually require proof of who you are. This can be a driver's license, passport, or any other form of ID. The website will let you know what IDs they will accept. They will also require proof of residence. This is usually through some sort of mail at your address. Most of the time, it is a utility bill. Some banks may require more. For example, USAA requires proof of your connection to the military. Always follow the guidelines of the bank you decided on.

Chapter 8: Negotiating Late Fees, Having a Plan, and Handling Credit Cards

I think everyone would agree, late fees are not fun. So many people would rather pay the late fees instead of doing something about them. When you find yourself in a situation that involves late fees, it does not help you to obtain financial freedom. Instead, it creates another debt or issue that hinders your freedom from obligations. Sometimes, it may even cause heartache or distress. Many people just pay fees to avoid these pains and frustrations. The one thing you do not realize is how they start to add up. If you are consistently paying these late fees, you may have given the bank over hundreds of dollars for free.

All it takes is for a phone call to handle these fees. Why pay the banks and give away your money when you can pay yourself? One of these fees could be as much as $35. When you think about it, that $35 can add up to a lot of money. All it takes to handle these fees is a phone call. These companies want you to call and manage them. The longer you wait, the harder it will get to negotiate the fees and possibly get out of them completely.

Talking Your Way Out of Fees

The question is, *"what do you tell them?"* I am going to give you a simple script that will help. Keep in mind, you may need to adapt to what the representative says to get what you need. The longer you wait, the bigger the fee could be. If the fees get too big, it will affect your credit score, and you may still need to pay a portion of the fees. I advise practicing this script several times before making the call. I would also make a list of things the representative may say and your response. I cannot tell you exactly what may happen in the conversation; however, I can help you be better prepared for every situation.

You: Hello, I am sorry! I just noticed I missed a payment. I was not aware it was due. I want to confirm that my credit score will not be affected.

Note: Your credit score is fundamental to your financial freedom. You will always want to say sorry that you did not know about the payment or whatever caused the fees.

Representative: Let me check the system and see what is going on. No, it will not affect your credit if you can take care of it in the next couple of days. However, there is a late fee, and by our policy, that fee will accumulate each day until it is paid.

Note: Usually, if you take care of your bill that you missed a payment on within a few days, it usually is not reported to any of the credit agencies. Always call to make sure.

You: Thank you! I am very grateful that it will not affect my credit score. I understand I was late on my payment, but could I would like to waive the fee.

Representative: Why would you like the fee waived?

You: It was my mistake, and it will not happen again. I would like to have the fee removed.

Note: You will always want to end this sentence with strength. Do not let it sound weak by saying, "can you...;" instead, say, "I would like...." You will seem more confident and increase your chances of getting the fee removed.

Representative: I very sorry, but I cannot remove the fee.

Note: At this point, the representative will try to get you to try something new. It is interesting, you have late fees, and they want you to add something to your service. That usually means they can do more than they say.

You: I am sorry! I have been using your company for several years. I would hate to go to a competitor because of this late fee. It would be a shame to lose a customer over this matter. I would like to ask if we can waive the late fee?

Representative: Hold on, let me check again. I am sorry for the wait and the inconvenience this has caused. I was able to waive the fee at this time, and it will be credited back to your account. Is there anything else I can help you with?

Note: Sometimes, the representative may still come back and tell you they cannot do it. Most of the time, they can do it at their level. However, some companies will not allow them to do it. It is ok to ask for a supervisor and ask them to handle it.

You did it. It really is that easy. You just need to pick up the phone and call. There was one time I called a company and used this script for a late fee. It worked like a charm. They also gave me $50 off on my next bill. They do not want their customers to go with a competing company. Their goal is to retain its customers. Anytime they lose a customer, they lose money.

Through this simple script, you can save thousands of dollars every year on late fees.

Avoiding Late Fees

The best way to save money on late fees is by avoiding them altogether. We can use financial planning to help us with this. Everything we do, we plan for it. When it comes to your money, you should expect and stick to it. That means if you have bills due, get them paid on time. Avoid those fees.

Most companies impose fees if it is not paid before the next bill is released. Therefore, that gives you extra time to ensure the bills are paid. However, watch out for those companies who imposed the late fee right away on your account. These accounts need to be monitored even closer.

Handling Credit Cards

Credit cards are a big one that imposes fees or interest at the new billing cycle. Everyone has a credit card. I personally do not like them. People think having a credit card gives them extra money when they do not have any. Therefore, they overspend and only make the minimum payments. They think, *"if I make the minimum payment, it is ok. At least the credit card is getting paid."* This is the wrong way of thinking.

Every credit card applies interest to the next billing cycle. When you pay the minimum balance, you are getting your payments made on time. It does show you are actively making payments on time. This is reflected in your credit score and shows good standing. However, eventually, it negatively affects your score. You will want to use your credit cards, but never max them out. Always use a minimum of 10% of your credit in credit cards.

You will want the credit bureaus to see you are using the credit responsibly given to you. When you max them out, you are showing you are not responsible. Also, think about all that interest you are paying by only paying the minimum balance. That is a lot of money you are giving away for free to the credit card companies.

Here is the secret that I use and save hundreds of dollars. I do not use the credit card if I do not have the money to pay it in full. When the credit card statement comes out, it is sent to the credit bureaus. Great, now it shows on the credit score. That will help you. Now you pay the bill on time and in full to confirm it is paid off on the next billing cycle. This will show responsibility for your credit.

Here is my second little secret. Find a credit card that offers cashback. Let your credit card make you money. You need to make payments on all your bills. Put them onto the credit card. You free up that money to help you through the month. When the statement comes out, pay the bill. All your monthly bills are paid. You will also earn cashback for every transaction you made with the credit card. This money can go back into your pocket.

In some cases, you may get enough cash back that paid for all your bills. The best credit card I have found is the Cosco credit card. It does come with a membership. However, you can get enough cash back on it if you use the credit card to pay off all your bills, your membership, and still have over $500 in your pocket. That is more than a $500 profit for using the credit card.

If you find the right card for you and your needs, make it work for you. It is possible to earn money from spending money. It is a great tactic to help you get out of debt and find yourself in financial freedom.

Chapter 9: Outsourcing to Virtual Job and All You Need to Know

Life tends to get business when you are running your own business. You may even say hectic. One of the best ways to help you with your company is outsourcing jobs. Sometimes you have tasks that need to be done that you cannot see a reason to hire someone to do; for example, a bookkeeper if that is their only job, and they only need to do it once a month. You would not hire a person to work one day a month to ensure your finances are straight. Let us see how this works.

Virtual Jobs

Not all people know the definition of the term "**virtual job,**" but if you look it up, some of the words that will prompt you are virtual, remote, at home, online job, distributed, or telecommuted jobs. A virtual appointment is a definition of a job done outside of a traditional office setting. These are the type of situations that are used to describe work-at-home employment or freelancing.

Typically, any person who works in a remote destination such as abroad, local coffee shops, or even the comforts of home can be called a virtual assistant. These types of people specialize in freelancing, or working on a contractual basis, with no boss, and no office.

Simply put, a digital nomad. They are the boss of themselves, and they hold their time off work. They can be employed in as many jobs as they can. We all want this kind of set-up. Have you probably imagined working in this type of setting? Most people only dream of working from home and not needing to out all the time.

As an employer or a businessman, hiring part-timers to work remotely or freelancers for a specific project will help you reduce costs. I will help you understand the definition, the purpose, and the uses of hiring a virtual assistant. You will determine the factors and areas that a virtual assistant does. Things you need to know so you can hire one, and if you are concerned about hiring an assistant to work from home job, you must know and understand the terminology, so you will then know how to make it work.

The duties of every virtual assistant vary depending on each industry and specific field. The good thing is you can always find one! Take a look at the definition of the term "virtual assistant" and help yourself to all the information I can provide. This might be overwhelming at first, but take one step at a time and gradually work your way down. As soon as you make the decision to try, you are already taking one step forward.

What is a Virtual Assistant?

The word "virtual" means online. A virtual job is anything work-related and done online with access through the internet. These jobs are done in a remote setting with no conditions of a boss, management, or a physical office.

These are mostly telecommuted, which means it does not require physical interaction but rather more online and provides flexible hours.

They are also called Virtual PA, Virtual Office Assistant, or only as V.A. Sometimes, they are being referred to as outsourced or freelancers. They come in all shapes and sizes. They are self-employed workers who specialize in different variety of services such as administrative works, technical support, customer service, writing, communication, and a health advocate. This type of work varies differently from each other. There are a host of things VA's do, such as social media management, email management, etc.

They mainly offer business support with tasks and projects remotely and can assist with a variety of day to day tasks. This is a person who provides support services to businesses, entrepreneurs, and brands from a different set location on an hourly rate or per a contract basis. They may work from the comforts of home, in a coffee shop, or even from a vacation rental. This type of work setting has become more popular with the influence of technology and social media. More and more people recognize these jobs, for it serves more comfort and convenience to the working community.

How Does a Virtual Assistant Work?

Virtual assistants become more significant as small businesses and startups companies start to rely on virtual offices to reduce the cost of workers and working hours while maintaining the quality of work.

Virtual assistants make use of technology and the internet to provide their services. Most often, they are on a contract basis. They look for clients who need their assistance in a specific field. They sign up on a working website, for example, Upwork.com, and post a listing for VA's who have talent and willingness to work on a client's contract arrangement.

Simple procedures include creating an account on the website, uploading their resume and sample of their work, and looking for clients or contracts. Every site has their onboarding process; some of them have a whole process which takes less than a couple of hours. Tenured VA's receive more contracts and established themselves as the credible assistant to make clients come looking for them rather than the other way around.

However, virtual assistants are on a contract basis, an independent contractor only meaning they do not get to have full access to employee benefits such as healthcare, insurance, and other compensations. The length of their contract may vary depending on the number of jobs a client offers them. They settle their paychecks online and receive them once they submitted a finished project.

VAs work mainly offsite, which means there is no need for a desktop, a computer, or other things a workforce needs. They primarily work in a more convenient setting than those full-time employees. Their work setup can include the most comfortable place they could be. Unlike in an office setting, they do not need to dress appropriately to report for work and no need for clockwork duty. They hold their working time in their hands so long as they finished their projects on or before the deadlines. Yet, to be able to work as one, they produce their computer or desktop equipment, purchase their software programs, and should have high-speed internet service.

What Can a Virtual Assistant Achieve?
There is a wide range of duties that a virtual assistant can perform. Most people who engage in this type of work uses their previous occupation to look for clients. Depending on their expertise and skills, they are hired by clients to complete a specific project. The duties and responsibilities of each VA vary according to the terms and regulations set by their contract. The following are some of the many jobs a virtual assistant can perform:

- Email management
- Answering calls
- Data Entry
- Planning and scheduling meetings
- Technical Support
- Bookkeeping
- Web developer
- Market research
- Graphic designing
- Blog management

- Transcription
- Event planning
- And so much more

There are all sorts of jobs and industry a virtual assistant can do. They are sometimes referred to as *"umbrella"* workers, which they're so many assistants and specialists that offer a range of services.

What Tasks Can You Outsource to a VA?

The number of jobs falls under the capacity of each VA can do is endless. Since they have the flexibility of time and for contracts, they absolutely can perform any task provided to them. I narrow down into three categories of what tasks you may use a VA for.

Business Administration: This is likely the things a secretary, personal assistant, or office manager can do. All this can be done remotely, such as booking meetings, organizing travels, emails, diary management, digital organizing, and a whole lot more!

Design: This falls under the technical work category. Since each design is unique, you will pay much higher than other lines of work. If you are starting or re-modeling, you need to have someone to create the logo of your company, your website, stationery, and other personalize things you need, such as flyers, business cards, and other merchandise.

Look for VA, who considers their line of work as their passion. Be on the lookout for a VA, who are putting a personal touch to their work, as this will make your investment worth it.

Marketing: This is what most VA can do. Several VA's had either had an experience in this field or probably work with a sales and marketing department before. Individual work can be on the field of content writing, blogging, email campaigns, and so many other tasks that take a lot of time and dedication that you just do not have. Consider working with someone that has a unique set of skills, so you do not feel like you are throwing your money away.

When to outsource a Virtual Assistant: From the employer's perspective, when there is a task that only requires a few hours per work each day, then it is impractical to hire someone full-time. For instance, a businessperson that handles too much work like managing emails and setting up appointments take a lot of burdens and may consider hiring a virtual assistant. Outsourcing a virtual assistant may very well be the best step to take for you to reach your personal and professional goals. Here are some of the many reasons you may consider outsourcing a virtual assistant.

- The business is starting to grow, but you arere planning for an expansion. This may need a consultation from an expert.
- You are burden with too much work and feel like there are never enough hours in a day.
- You are becoming restless and getting mixed up with your work.

- You need someone to do your administrative work

Business is always looking for cost-effective ways to do the routine task without sacrificing quality. However, there are also pros and cons to hiring a virtual assistant.

What are the Advantages of Hiring a Virtual Assistant?

Reduced Cost: This is Lower Salaries and Operating Expenses and Lower training costs.

Increase efficiency by reducing the workload: Since your assistant has their workspace with a full set of equipment and their powered technological gadgets. You will reduce your expenses, the cost of equipment, etc. and do not need extra office space. Also, more things get to be done since they can work at their own time, plus given the different time zone, you get to have finished jobs delivered once you woke up! It is that easy.

Flexible working time: They are working on their time basis, depending on the deadline you gave them as long as you provide the details on when and how you wanted the job done.

What Are Some Disadvantages With Hiring a VA?

There is less physical contact, which means the response time can be intermittent or take longer.

There is not enough control with how your assistant is doing the job since they are working in a different place, how can you sure that they are working and not playing.

They are Non-permanent staff and may lose motivation quickly.

Paying per contract means explaining the company's background with every new hire.

How Can I Spot a Good Virtual Assistant?

Now that you figured out the task and responsibilities of what a virtual assistant can be, it is time to move forward on how to spot a good VA. There are different sources of hiring a VA, especially when you are on new grounds. Manage your way through the internet, make use of different websites with utilizing platforms for VA jobs and Google searches.

In hiring a VA, make sure you post the most important and valuable skills and qualities you need in your business. Listed below are some of the classes a Virtual Assistant should have:

- Flexible
- Hardworking
- Impeccable time management
- Problem Solver
- Great communication skills
- Organized

- Reliable
- Resourceful

In line with this, you may also opt-out for a Non-Disclosure Agreement to protect yourself and your business. You may also want to perform a little background check and ask a couple of things from the VA; such as:

- ➤ Do you have any reviews?
- ➤ Are you registered with the ICO?
- ➤ Have long have you been a VA?

How Much Would a VA Typically Cost, and is that the Best Choice?

Hiring a virtual assistant and paying them should be an investment and must be an asset to your business. It is a new line item in your budget and a further expense to account for. Also, as an employer, before hiring a VA, you ask if they will add quality to your business. Since outsourcing is considered an investment, getting a higher return in good condition of work submitted within the deadline must be a priority. Working with a VA falls under a contract basis only, which limits you the option of paying employee's benefits or other legal obligations. Talk about another way to reduce costs!

One significance is every client, and assistant working relationship is unique. Every business is as individual as its owner.

There is no standard rate for a part-time or full-time virtual assistant. However, hiring support costs largely depend on various core factors. Also, there are several options for every client can consider when hiring support.

The Type of Work They Do
Since VA is considered as umbrella workers meaning they can be at a different industry at a different level, then they can do an enumerable variety of work. Below are the types of work a VA can do. The money you pay to your VA depends on the services you are getting from them. For example, hiring a secretary who will handle your calls and schedule appointments could cost you around $8 to $12 an hour.

Besides, make sure you look for a VA that fits the profile of somebody you are looking for. Every work comes with different prices. Perhaps administrative actions pay around $10-20 per hour; administrative services such as preparing business proposals, etc. vary from $30-40 per hour; in the meantime, specialized or technical jobs may charge higher than other contracts.

The Experience they have Before and Working as a VA
The conditions of hiring a VA can be the same in hiring an actual employee. The pay rate becomes higher when it comes to experience level since having years of experience are more efficient and already established a routine in beating deadlines. Usually, a VA with a lot of experience will charge more.

However, you may opt for a VA with less experience who charges less for their services. Just make sure the quality of their work will not be affected by their inexperience. Some of the best ways to prevent this are to ask for a sample of their work before hiring them or send them a copy of the work you wanted to be done. Judge them through their character and attitude; considering, all the best employees come with the best practical approach.

The size and deadline of the contract between the VA and the employer: The contract should include the scope of the work and the timelines your VA should submit their work. Sometimes the more difficult the agreement is, the higher the payment a VA requires. Administrative work should cost less than technical tasks. However, the rate of pay still depends on the employer-assistant contract. Again, each owner is different and makes each rate pay unique.

Their location formwork: Virtual assistants also vary based on the country's location. Most contractors and employers chose to hire VA who are coming from India and the Philippines since they charge cheaper rates. This is also brought about by the currency exchange rate of their countries. For example, a typical American business person will look for VA in the Philippines and will only need to pay $6 per hour; which, is converted to Philippines' currency and is equivalent to a one-day 8-hour shift for them. Investing in a VA from these countries ensure your money back and saves you more cost.

There are hourly bulk packages you can purchase as an agreement or create your package so long as it fits the needs you decide upon with the VA. The cost of a VA boils down to several factors.
- The level of experience
- The number of projects/tasks you want them to complete
- The budget you are willing to dispose of

Besides, each contract comes with a risk, since you are paying a virtual person, the risk of quality work can be the sacrifice. Yet everything still depends on you as an employer.

What Tools Increase the Effectiveness of Your VA?
Since you are employing someone that you cannot meet in person and have a different time zone than you, there is a need to have a system that will align you and your assistant when it comes to working issues. You need to create a project management system that will manage your project by planning, organizing, and maintaining its different aspects. This is one way to create a genuinely capable, organized team. It allows you to assign tasks, set dates, and create your style of communication means.

You will be creating a uniform set of tools and file servers where you will upload files and projects in one place, making it easier to refer to later. The manufacturing of this system organizes your plans and align the goals of your business with your VA. It pays to create a shared network.

This will facilitate all your needs to your contracted VA despite the diversity and different locations you are both in. An example of which is the online Dropbox folder or Google Drive, which gives you the same access to all files, accounts, or software programs you will be needing.

A shared system drive is a great place where updates and feedback can be stored without duplication. This way, the employer can specify which task needs to finish, and the VA can note which ones have already been completed.

In addition to this, you can also make use of the different social media platforms and applications that promote and makes communication the easiest. There is a variety of them; including, Facebook messenger, Viber calls and messaging, Zoom Teleconference, and more. Plus, these are for free and accessible anytime through the Internet. Being comfortable on the phone meant that you could readily suggest other time-saving systems or flag potentials issues.

If you have no experience working with this type of system before, you will likely stumble upon one. You will find yourself using the system on a professional and personal level. In some cases, your virtual assistant may have used one already, so they should be able to walk you through it or recommend one for you.

How to Work with a VA? Do This!

There are a few things you should consider when working with a VA.

Trust Your VA
Trusting your VA means putting and sharing a portion of your business in their hands. Trusting them does not only fall in hiring them for their expertise but also allowing them to exercise integrity and initiative in completing their projects. Giving them the benefit of the doubt that they will deliver above your expectations.

Give Clear Instructions to What You Need
One way to be successful in hiring VA's is to provide clear instructions with the content of your goals. Also, become transparent to them with the things you wanted to achieve. If you do not provide clear instructions, the task may not meet your expectations, and your VA will not understand what you need to complete.

To achieve these goals, you can create a detailed list of instructions with every task a VA may need to do. This may be time-consuming, but it is well worth it on the back end with saving time and fewer mistakes, but sure is worth it.

Inform Your VA of Your Priorities
Through being transparent of the goals, you want to achieve, you are guiding your VA to deliver the work that suits your business best. Without clear priorities, it is challenging to manage your time and make progress with your goals. You will become overwhelmed by trying to take on too many responsibilities.

The ability to move forward with your VA and accomplish your goals together often depends on what you decide to prioritize. Be clear with the things you need to have first; this will set the pace for your VA to start and, most importantly, paves the way for a good working relationship for both of you.

Be Patient

Due to many differences between you and the VA, small conflicts or disagreement could happen. There might be one or two items that you and your VA differ entirely. Perhaps it could be your beliefs, your upbringing, your culture, or work ethics. These factors can contribute to little disagreements, which could then result in a conflict.

Being patient with your VA can bring a lot of positive effects on your projects and maybe create more in the future. Try to give one task at a time and manage your expectations for whatever your VA is doing. Be patient, polite, and gracious to your VA.

Use the Right Tools

Using the right tool can make your life easier and speed up the completion of each project. Also, it will help strengthen the process of communicating with them and training the new ones. Make use of applications that are for free yet offer the best of your business interest. Apps such as Dropbox or Evernote are designed for easy access to files and information, Jing or Screener, to create online video tutorials for quick, on-the-job training. These tools are all available online, and some of them are even free! Make use of them!

Be Kind

Being a problematic boss will not get you anywhere. Sometimes it pays to be kind too. Virtual assistants are people also, and they will always be more than willing to do the work you asked them to do if you treat them with respect and kindness. There are a lot of ways on how to be kind to your VA. For example, if they submitted a project before their deadline, pay them extra, or perhaps make them your regular VA. These are one of the many ways on how you can exercise kindness to your VA. You will never know that extra money you give turns out to be the payment for the medical expenses of your VA's family member. Being kind inevitably creates a difference.

Over-Communicate

To document everything and scheduling daily one-on-one meetings. You will want to create an environment that is safe for you and your VA. Through a safe environment, your VA will be willing to reach out when they have questions. Keep asking if they are having problems or not. Regularly repeat yourself with every project goal you have with your VA and reiterate the things that need to be done first. As an employer, it is your responsibility to articulate an effective strategy that is communicated clearly and consistently to your VA. Provide a shared direction for both of you to move fast and focus on matters the most.

Be Realistic

Set a practical limit to what your VA can do and going to be able to accomplish without ever meeting or seeing your business. Do not set impossible deadlines and projects. Perhaps try testing your VA with different tasks that vary from simple to complex projects and get an idea of how they are capable and able to deliver. Let them define their weakness or limitations to align your goals to the deliverance of a project. Set your working relationship on the confinements of your goals and what your VA can deliver. Also, try to be positive despite every challenge.

Invest Your Time

Investing your time means being always available to your assistant. Whenever they ask for help or questions that are work-related, give them the time that they need or better yet invest more time for them. Once you do this, your assistant will be more than willing to do the task you want them to do. Engage in activities that provide positive results and focus yourself on helping them as much as you can. Value the things they do and try to celebrate their progress. This way, you are building a relationship with the people who matter in your business and, at the same time, receiving higher returns of your money.

Let Them Ask Questions

For some, asking questions takes time, that it is easier to tell them what to do. In many ways, asking questions had a more significant impact than asking people to do things. As an employer of these virtual assistants, you also serve as their mentor. Especially with a new VA, they want to understand the world of working virtually, how it all works, and how to interact with employers such as you. Asking questions has its benefits such as questions reveal interest, it gaps the strength of understanding; it improves recalling information they receive, and items that make a VA engaged.

Have open communication with your virtual assistant, let them feel free to ask for clarification or guidance at any time without hesitation. This will reduce the chance of work being redone and prevents you from wasting more time than it should.

How to Work with a VA? Do Not Do This!

We just talked about things you should do when working with a VA. However, like all good things, there are also wrong. Do not do these with a VA.

Do Not Micromanage Your VA

Put your mind at ease and expect things to be done with little or no errors. For some, micromanaging may be a way for management to make sure tasks are performed in a precise manner. The problem is, it is not always the right or most productive way of doing things.

You might think gaining control is an effective way to manage your people, yet not always. Gaining too much control over your people will eventually lead to a massive breakdown of trust between you and them. When trust is gone, there can be a loss of productivity and loss of VA signing up for you.

Keep in mind, the people you hired are professionals in a specific industry, the only difference from before and now is the work setting and location. Nevertheless, these people are experts in their particular field and only signed up for a contract they know how accomplished. Stop asking for regular progress reports, instead critic them once they are done. Trust them enough that they will deliver on what was agreed upon. When you micromanage them, you are telling them that you don't trust them. Have confidence in their actions and decisions in producing excellent results.

Do Not Forget to Set Deadlines

Be transparent enough to inform your VA about your deadlines and strictly implement completion before payment. This may be an advantage on their side, for they tend to become stress getting things done as the deadline is approaching. However, reiterating the importance of the period can be a powerful tool, especially if you know how to use it properly. Deadlines can help you clearly explain your goals, increase both your productivity and taking control of your work, which will produce a positive result.

Work your deadlines with your VA. Set realistic terms and conditions for your VA, be flexible, and be kind enough to provide deadline extensions or other options. This prevents burnout on your VA, stress, limits the errors, and keeps the VA from redoing their work.

The freedom your VA enjoys as a freelancer comes with tradeoffs. It is for them to understand that every contract they signed up for comes with a particular deadline. However, these deadlines were not meant to scare them slightly to push them to do the best of their ability to get the job done. Make them grasp the idea that deadlines do not have to be viewed as ticking time bombs, which intends to control their lives. Instead, timelines can be used to jumpstart their creativity, productivity, and manage their time effectively.

Do Not Ignore Your VA
One of the factors that push people in business from hiring a VA is to lessen the burden of work. It is tempting to think that once they hire a VA, they can just delegate the work and come back for them once they are done. However, this mindset is not as effective as it sounds. As an employer, you need to set up a time to review everything they do so you can determine problems and provide suggestions, lessening the chances of errors, and redoing their work.

Keeping in contact with your VA can help a lot. Constant communication can raise productivity and work efficiency between the two of you. A regular phone call allows you to keep track of your VA's progress; it also delegates tasks well and providing your VA a chance to suggest other ways to save time.

Always be on the lookout for the needs of your VA. Let them know that in-between deadline, and you are willing to help. Set a constant communication with your VA to let them know that you are always available. In some cases, you take no notice of them, make sure to contact them back once you are within reach. It is easy to get busy and forgot your VA temporarily, but if you want them to be effective, give at least a portion of your time to them. This way, they will likely become productive and efficient.

Responsibilities of a VA

There are several responsibilities you may assign to a VA. Always be mindful of what your VA knows how to do. You would but assign a writer to create a database or a web designer to write a blog post.

Since the world's extensive use of the internet has progressed, the number of virtual assistant services has significantly grown. The number of people giving up their corporate office to work in the comforts of their home as a virtual assistant has become massive. More and more people engage in freelancing, as it yields innumerable benefits. Such as flexible hours, remote working, competitive pay, and the unique ability to choose the clients they work with. Another advantage of freelancing is the ability to choose their workload. They can work with projects as little as they want or as many as they can so long as it could be delivered with the deadline. The idea is you get a focus on your work without the hindrance of a full-time job like meetings, office politics, office noise, and distractions.

The availability of virtual jobs online is everywhere. Try looking for websites that have contract listings, and you will see countless of jobs posted online. A small business owner hires a virtual assistant will trim off-hours from their workweek. This will add to a long line of benefits such as no more needing to pay an employee-related expense, no separate office space, no worries concerning downtime, and no morale to be raised.

Since it is contract-based, you simply pay that VA for the services they delivered as in line with their contract's arrangement. However, since these services still involve a human workforce, it is always important to treat a VA like a full-time employee. There should be trust and dependability between the both of you. This way, VAs become significant to your business organization and will likely bring your business to progress.
Having a VA will have its good and bad points.

As an SBO, be mindful of the disadvantages the come along with hiring a VA. For instance, there are some instances that they cannot deliver the projects accurately as you want them to be. For some reason, due to inconsistent culture, location, language barriers, and other differences, it hinders them from completing a project thoroughly.

Understanding the kind of person your VA could help you to identify the type of projects you will be assigned to them. For instance, if they are good at writing, then you can assign them content writing assignments, or perhaps some of them are good in making a marketing plan, then you can assign them all the technical aspects of your business. By doing so, you are delegating the right task to the right person, which increases the chance for your business to grow.

As you focus on the growth of your company, VAs will do the things you are not supposed to be doing. As you manage the whole public stage of your business, your VAs are on the background running the show, saving you more time for running errands.

Responsibility: General Virtual Assistance
Also known as GVA, which fundamentally does the same work as a personal assistant, secretary, and office administrator. The only difference between them and the VA is how the work is delivered. Their work mostly comprised of administrative work such as email management, scheduling appointment, book appointments with clients, etc.

When hiring this type of VA, you need to let them grasp the idea of them aligning their time difference to your time zone and work schedule. You need to train them according to your business policies, systems, and process. It is an advantage if you can hire someone who has experience in your field. You might have to provide them the tools and software similar to the ones you are using. Overall, working with General Virtual Assistant may prompt you to arrange a comprehensive training plan. This may appear as a long process, but once you have the right human resources fit for the work, it will reduce your business expenses along with lessening your burden of work.

VGA work is mostly consisting of administration emails, payrolls, invoicing, sales reports, and customer inquiries. Through finishing each of these tasks, most entrepreneurs can increase productivity and help small business soar to new heights.

Here are the duties and responsibilities of a General Virtual Assistant:

- Bookkeeping and payroll duties which include calculating hours, adding expenses, and updating salaries.
- Receptionist duties such as answering calls, leaving voicemails, and checking messages.
- Entry and updates of data.
- Performing banking needs, including paying bills and transferring funds (Transactions are mostly done online).
- Creating, filling, and presenting weekly reports on sales, deliverables, hours, and tasks.
- Email management, responding to customer inquiries, and managing spam mails.
- Involving in chat support and organizing technical support.
- Creating and sending greeting cards and other personal notes.
- I was managing a calendar of important events.
- Scheduling appointments with clients and other business people.

- Managing online accounts and share drives such as DropBox, OneDrive, and Google.
- I was working with files, including PDF files and Microsoft Programs.
- Proofreading documents and other office materials.

Responsibility: Content Writing

Content Writing is the process of planning, writing, and editing web content. This is an art form that cannot be performed by everyone, as this is done only by experts in journalism and marketing. Professionals in this field plan and execute a content campaign making it more meticulous. Hiring a virtual assistant in this field should have at least a long experience of being a content writer.

An excellent content writer will know how to write to a target audience, create an outline to publish, connect to the public, and create statements that will either make or break your business. Therefore, hiring somebody with years of experience in content marketing or have been writing in blogs for too long, can generate a minimum of 200 words per post, with the knowledge of using social media and other internet resources and have at least contributed articles for videos, blog post, and other media relation materials. Hiring the right people to do the job will make your life easier and produce positive results for your business.

It is an advantage to hiring a virtual content writer. However, you must be mindful of some things that can create an effect on your work. This includes the willingness and can work remotely, fluent in English, and with an outstanding knowledge of the English language. They must be able to work under pressure since it includes countless revisions and deadlines, with attention to detail, with the ability to work independently, multi-task, and meet deadlines.

Here are a few of the many duties of a content writer:

- They are creating articles and blog posts.
- Guest posting and guest blogging.
- Making press releases, newsletters, and submitting these to papers or designated areas.
- We are producing eBooks, white papers, and other content marketing materials such as infographics.
- I am designing brochures.

Responsibility: Search Engine Optimization (SEO) & Digital Marketing

Search Engine Optimization is a process of getting traffic to your website through the use of a search engine. By hiring an SEO, you will attract eyeballs and gain recognition to meet your business goals. A virtual assistant with experience in SEO or digital marketing will provide value to your company. Many times, when you look for a content writer, you also want someone who can SEO their articles as they write.

The right VA will enhance web traffic, sales numbers, and make your brand public. SEO specialist reviews analyze and create changes to websites, so they are being optimized for search engines. As a specialty, it is their job to place your site at the top of the search engine results. Since this type of work mostly falls under technical service, they should be a problem solver and decision-maker.

Some of their responsibilities may include:

- Developing, updating, optimizing SEO, and web marketing strategy.
- Supervise keyword research for a website.
- They are creating and setting up a landing page.
- We are establishing an in-depth competitor analysis.
- Off-page optimization, participating in internet forums, and message boards.
- Monitoring and observing traffic in Google Analytics reports.
- We are designing advertisements to be sent out to the public.
- Produce a new list of email contacts, email newsletters, and promotional copy.

Responsibility: Social Media

As time progresses and modernization advances, the role of social media has become vital to the growth of every business. Putting your business online is the same as advertising your products for free. Having a presence on social media will put your brand out there for more people to see it. It is better to have one than not have one at all.

Marketing on social media will involve some meticulous planning. With a VA, you can designate several tasks to them. Hiring a virtual assistant to manage these aspects of your business can bring good and positive improvements to your business.

They can pitch more ideas, set up and organize your presence in the online world, do some research, ensure the consistency of your online business post, create online content, and publish blog posts. Also, hiring a VA with prominent social media accounts will understand how to get noticed, retweeted, or shared in every social media account. This type of VA will likely put your business in the spotlight.

In most recent times, more companies have been growing their social media spending by 70 percent. Mobile marketing had been significant in making a business boom. With a large amount being dispensed in this area, you do not want to waste more than your labor expenses.

As a businessman, you may think that managing social media accounts is accessible to everyone. Yet, it is not and could eat up a massive amount of your time, so better to save money and time hiring a VA and leaving it to them.

Here are some of the many responsibilities a Social Media Virtual Assistant can do:

- Creating and updating social media accounts such as Facebook, Twitter, Google+, Instagram, etc. regularly
- Editing detailed profiles and polishing them by inserting links of your company websites.
- Generate a content creation strategy.
- Perform social media audits: conduct a thorough analysis of traffic, shares, and mentions.
- Optimize a full strategy for each small business mobile social media.
- Make your business trending by using hashtags for the day that fits for the company.
- You are strengthening your business relationship through excellent customer service such as responding to inquiries, sharing relevant information, thanking customers for mentions, and purchases.
- Develop a marketing strategy by running a media contest, challenge, etc.

Responsibility: Web Developing

In the modern world, pretty much everyone has access to the internet, and a massive percentage of people are using the internet almost every single day. By placing your business on the internet radar, you will likely receive favorable outcomes. Thus, online marketing is a tool every person in business should consider.

Online marketing is an effort to spread the word about your business that makes use of the internet to reach people. It is everything you do online to target your audience and create a name for your business, so you are known. At some point making people want to become your customers. One great example of this online marketing is to create a website for your business.

Your VA should have the skills necessary to produce a website suited for your liking. However, a VA should have experience in coding, creating HTML, and exquisite programming. Channel your ideas in your head to a web developer. Teamwork with your VA will help create an outstanding website that clearly shows people what your business is about.

Be mindful of the following traits your website should have:

- Fast loading times.
- All ages navigate easy usability and can.
- Contains all of your business information and contacts.
- Almost everyone with no problem can navigate it.
- It can be found on top of the list in a search engine.

Here are a few of the responsibilities of a Web Developer:

- Creating a website utilizing planning, designing, and developing a program.
- They are providing technical support through coding.

- Installing, customizing, and updating WP plug-ins and themes.
- Researching different software programs and maintaining software documentation.
- Creating and managing a back-up plan in case the website goes down.
- They are maintaining regular back-ups to prevent data loss.
- Has an ability to multi-task within time constraints, budgets, and business goals.
- Strong communication skills with other colleagues in the business to develop and position their content.

Responsibility: Audio & Video Editing

Generally, creating quality video content is time-consuming and sometimes requires a full set of skills for doing this type of work. Since videos are an essential part of Social Media Marketing, promoting videos will help you achieve significant branding.

To escalate the quality of your videos attached to your website, enhance the use of the sound of your webinars or podcast, and make your social media stand out from the rest of the crowd in your niche; you need to hire an experienced video and sound editor.

Your virtual assistant will free up your time for other business management activities. These will reduce some costs and avoid buying expensive video editing software.

Here are some of the Virtual Assistant specialties in Video and Sound Editor:

- Basic video editing, such as creating explicit intros, outros, inputting graphics, and music to all of your videos on your websites.
- I was uploading these videos regularly.
- Edit existing footage and meeting your video standards.
- Add natural sounding audio effects to your video, making them more compelling.
- Trimming sound footage and setting up your podcast or webinars.
- I was editing images in Photoshop and other image editing software.

Responsibility: Miscellaneous

As a businessman, apart from managing essential things in your business, you also need to get some random stuff done. It could be anything from taking notes during meetings to buying items for your office. These tasks may seem little and small, but once they piled up, they can take a chunk of your time. After a while, you were starting to realize you are spending a lot of time on non-essential tasks, which can have serious after effect on the growth of your business.

Delegating these tasks to your personal VA will take the burden off your shoulder. These will help you manage your time and let you focus on a more productive purpose. Your

VA will perform these general tasks for you, which will allow you to save money on higher labor costs.

Some of the tasks they may perform are:

- Takedown notes and minutes from meetings and then create a detailed document.
- Producing voicemails, video or audio, podcast, and meeting recordings.
- Recruiting and hiring of potential team members and contracts that are essential to your business.
- I was researching relevant information and statistics, facts for meeting presentations.
- We are placing career ads on job sites and other hiring websites.
- Perform all the necessary recruitment, job hiring, and processing employee kits.
- We are changing raw data to reports and slideshows.
- We are arranging itineraries such as flight details, hotel bookings, transportations, and reservations.
- Perform human resource management work.
- Speaking with customer care representatives for solving and closing technical issues.
- Act as the overall customer service staff for your employer and taking care of all customer issues and concerns

Overall, having a virtual assistant can save you time and money. Let them do the jobs that you are not as skilled in while you focus on the part of the business you are experienced in.

Chapter 10: Ways to Travel More Without quitting Your Job and Still Be Financial Stable

Do you wish to travel more? Do you want to trade your current lifestyle to traveling but still want to keep your job? There are many different travel job opportunities to make money while traveling abroad. Also, you have a lot of options to take when you are looking to trade work for accommodation, or something essential to give you the freedom to travel abroad but at the same time keeping your job.

You have options! You decide! Here are a few ways that will point you in the right direction to get started. Remember traveling is not made for everyone, but if you are likely in shape and fit to do both work and travel, then maybe you meant to be a digital nomad after all. Just remember the basics and try following these rules!

Prioritize in Finding a Fast Internet Access

To continue working while traveling, you need to prioritize certain things, such as an internet connection. You should not compromise your direct communication with your employer to keep you from working. You must hold all the communication channels open and available. To do this, you must inform your host or accommodation ahead of time about your needs.

Let them be aware that aside from having a vacation, you are also there for work. Also, before choosing your place of liking, make sure to check the reviews regarding the things you need during your stay. If you come across a site with slow internet, consider moving elsewhere.

If the problem still exists, opt-out for other options such as purchasing a portable internet router, mobile data, or even look for a computer shop with a LAN connection. Vacation places with reliable internet connections are usually rare. These situations are made for relaxing and unwinding. Certain things, such as wifi, are deemed to be a distraction rather than a necessity.

Embrace Work and Play as the Same

The purpose of this endeavor is to take both traveling while working at the same time. It does not hurt if you traded your Monday look to a pair of swim shorts and a can of beer in one hand or perhaps make your lunch break longer than usual with a scenic view.

This could be you, or this could be somebody else. Yet you did not take this leap of faith just to stick at your same office doing the same routine wherever you are. Remember that one of the reasons most people work hard is because they wanted to travel. So it pays to have a good time once in a while. You deserve it!

Research Places to Work

If you get the chance to travel while working, make use of the opportunity by visiting some famous sites that are found in your location. Be one of the locals by placing your travel dates closer to their festivals, annual events, or maybe you may try eating their local foods while staying at one place. Travel away from the area you are visiting and discover all the things it could offer. Try to be productive in your work and, at the same time, have fun. You will never want to miss this kind of opportunity.

Be Clear with Your Manager or Clients

There is this notion that when it comes to working away from your corporate office means you are not working at all. However, this situation is far from the truth. If specific individuals were given this type of opportunity, they would not take the chance for granted.

The fear of losing a job is higher than the fear of not having the chance to travel. If you were only given a temporary grant to take your work along with your vacation dates, be clear to your boss or to your clients, so the expectations are clear. Inform them about the differences which could take place when your away while working; For example, the different time zone on how it might affect meetings, response time, or perhaps you will be in transit during office hours. Nevertheless, do not let this disrupt your productivity and lessen your value at work.

Be Wise About Housing

In finding your place to stay, make use of your resources such as technology and mobile application. There are apps with goals designed for working nomads. They have properties that offer all the necessities you need for working on the road. However, this might cost you more expensive than a regular traveler.

The importance of being wise about housing is it can help you save up money. Look for places that offer the things you need but at a lower price. You need to save up as much as you can since you are away from home, in a strange place, and posed as a foreigner. You will never know when an inevitable tragedy happens; therefore, it pays to be prepared.

Plan Your Travels Around Paid Holiday Weekends

Perhaps this is the easiest way to maximize your travel. Plan your trips around paid holidays, like reserving your weekends for starters. Then take a Monday and Tuesday off, thus creating four days of vacation with paid holidays, and you could make it even longer.

Take Shorter Trips During the Week to Maximize Your Vacation Time

Instead of using all your vacation leave at once, why not align it during weekends and take shorter trips. This way, you get to visit a couple of places instead of only one.

Make use of your weekends by visiting historical or tourist attractions located near you. Visit a city with only a two-hour flight away so you will not be missing out on something important such as work. After all, a vacation does not have to be long and far from home to be fun and enjoyable.

Things to Avoid

You are on vacation even though you will be working. Enjoy yourself! Here are a few things to avoid during your time away from the office.

Feeling Lonely

Since you are away from home, feeling homesick is one of the hard things you will have. It is tough to make new friends, especially when you are only there for a short time. Therefore, you need to develop some social skills, at least as you go along. Broaden your social network by checking in with your friends or relatives if they know someone in the place you are heading. Use this to create a connection, perhaps build a relationship with locals, so when you come back, you have someone to look forward to seeing. Feeling lonely usually happens at the start of your arrival; however, it will not last long as you adjust to your situation.

Working All the Time

One of the many disadvantages of bringing your work with you while you travel is when you are in a different time zone and need to extend a long time just to accommodate your office mates. This might be a hard thing at your end, but you have an option on how you react to it. If you have an hour to spare before catching a meeting, why not use it to visit a local shop or find an exhibition. This might not work at first since you will be opting for rest rather than going out; however, as you adjust, you might accommodate these options.

Bringing too Much Stuff
If you are working while traveling, you must be flexible all the time. This includes bringing lighter stuff and only what is necessary. Do not make your travel difficult by bringing along too much stuff. Remember, you will be moving from one place to another, and that means so is your luggage. Do yourself a favor by not giving yourself a hard time.

Spending Money Unwisely
Since you are in a strange place surrounded by unfamiliar faces, you might want to come prepared. Save up as much money you can, and this can help you in case of emergencies. Create a budget plan on how much you can spend on your daily meals, accommodation, and recreation. Stick to your budget always. Minimize penalties, know the value of your location currency, avoid withdrawing cash to lower transaction fees, and still learn how to judge scam transactions. Avoid buying things you do not need, especially if you are in the midst of your vacation. Recreational spending can be done days before leaving.

Reasons Why You Do Not Need to Quit Your Job

Traveling is nice. It is always nice to leave your office and explore the world or spend time with your family. However, can you afford to quit your job? Here are a few reasons why you should not leave for your travels.

Travel is Not Cheap

If you could travel while having to keep your job, do not take it for granted and be flexible enough to make it work. Just because you get to go while doing a job assignment does not mean you have to stop working.

Remember that traveling is not cheap, and living in a foreign place still needs sustaining, both financially and physically. It is not feasible to travel without an income. Even if you save up money for a long trip, it will eventually run out. Quitting your job while you are not financially stable is not a smart move.

Remote Work is Not for Everyone

Although many people want to be in a situation where they get to work while in the comforts of their home or in front of a view overlooking overlook some beautiful scenery, not everyone can do it. Doing remote work is not for everyone, for work still requires being on time for meetings, a specific number of hours per task, or work within a particular hour. The factors of every corporate office still exist in working remotely.

This may also be challenging in terms of focusing on work because being your boss can inhibit you from being distracted easily. Think about how distracted you can be when you browse Facebook in the middle of your work. Not so efficient after all! This is the reason some people still choose the comfort of an office rather than working away.

Long-Term Travel is Not for Everyone
Not everyone is cut out for long travel. It felt nice at first, but when you make it part of your living, you will realize that constant movement will wear you out and could be made you unhappy.

If you like a home base and familiar things to return to after being away for a while, then you are not made to travel long but rather could enjoy shorter trips. If you opt to work while going or perhaps move to a different country while continuing to work, then you need to make sure you can survive. Walking into a different place with most of the things different from where you have been can be daunting.

You Do Not Have to Travel to be Fulfilled
Not all people are cut out to visit just to see the world or perhaps explore to live your life or feel you have a purpose. The actual truth is you do not have to travel to be fulfilled because traveling is not a priority for everyone, and not everyone was made to move.

Traveling while working has its advantage and disadvantages. Depending on why you are going for work, your situations, and experiences will vary. There are a lot of factors that can either contribute or disrupt your job while you are traveling, and you need to evaluate them carefully first.

Remember, when choosing to work remotely, you may still be a full-time job—being able to work while on the move requires dedication, self-awareness, a tolerance for uncertainty, and flexibility. It means your focus is always going to be split. There is still a distraction when you work along, and this is a factor that will lessen your productivity.

However, the most important thing to do when you opt for this kind of lifestyle is to make sure you are prepared. Research your way in and out of your new place, know everything, find connection, and determine how to last long.

Although everything might be overwhelming at first, as you go through the steps, I have laid out for you and carefully apply it to your situation, and you will realize that juggling work and travel is fun all the time. Eventually, you will gain a better sense of how to make this lifestyle work for you.

Chapter 11: How to Achieve the Lifestyle You Designed

Lifestyle is the term that defines every person's way of life. This is a way of living for every individual, family, and society on a day-to-day basis. It is composed of a person's attitudes, habits, and moral standards brought together as a mode of living. This term is used to define the social status and the way of life of every person.

This is a reflection of a person's self-image or self-concept; generally, how they see themselves or how people see them, how they act towards others through their environment, the value of their money, and their social circle. Most people tend to judge a person through their lifestyle. Although, as you grow to become an adult, you will realize that a lifestyle is interchangeable, which means you have the option to change it, whether it is for the benefit of right or not.

We will compare your plan and progress to the action of building an actual house. The purpose of this reading is to get you acquainted with the things you wanted out of your life. We will use the metaphor of building a house to compare it to your progress.

In making a house, you start with a plan first, to create the blueprint of the house, to build it, and to see it finished. In a lifestyle change, you also need an idea, a series of actions, and a set of attitudes on how to make it work and achieve it.

You might find yourself overwhelmed with all the information provided to you. Nevertheless, it is always up to you on how you are going to make it work. Why not start with the decision to build the house, the lifestyle you want and slowly work your way up until you see it finished.

Decide on What You Want Out of Life

Start with identifying the things you wanted to change in your life and point out the way you want it to become. Do you want to lose more weight? Or live a healthier lifestyle? Fashionable? Or perhaps you wanted to become the image of a minimalist? These are only some of the lifestyles people are into.

Similar to building a house, you need to come up with the decision to make it first. You need to create a vision on how your home will turn out then consider it as your mission to finish it. Envision yourself to attain all your lifestyle goals. Imagine what you would become after the process is over? These are only some of the things you need to identify for you to jump in the process of changing lifestyle.

Decide on what you want out of life. This will help you focus on the things you want to do. This will set up the perimeter of the things that you need for you to reach your goals. You will position yourself on how to start changing your lifestyle.

The most important thing is for you to have the willingness to start and the motivation to come up with a plan. Start with checking in yourself, point out the things that outgrow you, or annoy you? What are the items you want to change for the better?

Look for the most important things you want to change about your life? Is it something that you do not want to do anymore? Either way, focus on one change at a time. Lifestyle change is a process; nothing successful happens overtime.

Start to Envision Your Life is Already How You Want It

Upon building a house, during the planning process, you start to identify the color of the façade you wish to show. What is the structure of the house? What is the design you want to follow? This time, planning had progressed to the building's layout and design. You are now envisioning the whole house itself, its appearance, its color, its design, and its structure.

Overall, the blueprint is completed. As a comparison, lifestyle change should include envisioning the kind of life you wanted to have. Creating a vision of your life will serve as the blueprint of your goals. Think of crafting your life's idea as mapping a path to the things you wanted to change and the kind of life you want. Experts and most life success stories started with an image.

Once you decided to start and make a change, it is about time to envision yourself in a better place than where you are now. Position yourself to the things you wanted to have, and then you will see items starting to move in the direction where you want it to be. Look for the differences in your life that may happen if you start changing your lifestyle.

Consider all your needs. Think about your personal and professional needs. It does not matter if your needs are tangible or intangible. They are just as important. Look for the reasons why you wanted to change your lifestyle. It may be helpful if you start writing down your thoughts, eventually creating your plan or try putting together a vision board.

Make this idea your blueprint. Allow yourself to dream and imagine a clear picture of living the lifestyle you want. Focus on how your best life would feel. Claim the life you wanted and risk everything you have when things start to fall off, and you are in no position to give up so easily.

Whatever you want to succeed in doing, you must first find the courage to start. Then you must continue doing it until all of the things you envisioned will turn out to be real.

Think About the Experiences that Make you Happy and Repeat Them

One of the fantastic things about building a home is once it finished, it does not bring you joy? Are you not glad that despite the hardships you have encountered, yet, it still turns out to be the home you want it to be? If you were to describe the happiest experience you ever had, what would you say? Does it feel good if you are always happy?

Most of the time, our actions are guarded by the thoughts that could make us happy. We try to do things that can make us happy as much as we can.

For you to continue what you had started, think about the experiences that make you happy, and repeat them. Focus yourself on what you would become. Live the life you want. When you are trying to figure out how to create the life you want, envision the experience that makes you truly happy and does those things as often as you can.

This can help you create positive thoughts and produce positive outcomes. For some, it could be spending more time with their children, or perhaps it is writing your thoughts on in a journal. However, to create a positive result, be mindful of continuing to do these actions to create a positive and happy life.

A lifestyle change may not be secure, and it takes a full amount of support and dedication to create a new habit. This can be an excruciating process that takes time and require more self-dedication. Try changing one behavior at a time.

Start with thinking carefully about every experience that makes you happy, create a pattern of behavior that fits you, and repeats this pattern until they are wired to your brain. Although this is not a quick process and it is not easy, but our brain works fast on what makes us succeed so we can repeat it.

Become Goal-Oriented

Being goal-oriented means being selfish in your ways; it means that you need to figure out precisely what you want. Look out for yourself first and set your targets and objectives that will make progress in making your life much smoother. Focus on yourself before anything else and work towards achieving your goals. For most people, their achievements are connected to their habits.

To pull off the lifestyle you want depends on the quality of habits you have, which will determine how successful you can become. Thus, one of these habits you must practice it to be a goal-driven person.

In constructing a house, you need to have a goal of finishing it, which is similar to possessing the lifestyle you wanted to have. Somehow the happy life you have envisioned is tied up in attaining all of your goals.

You need to be motivated enough to keep trying new ways until all of your goals are met. Do you always want to have that fit body? Set up regular schedules at the gym or eat healthier meals. Want to be financially independent? Start setting aside money. Set aside time for mastering skills if you want a specific job. Immerse yourself to the vision you created and imagine that you have already achieved that goal in the future.

Think about the goals, and you can complete them faster. Practice mental focus to get closer to the life you wanted to have. Combine this vision with mediation and a positive outlook. These are some of the many goals you can set up to yourself.

To be successful in achieving this, you should take care of the task at hand and continually moving forward. Do not procrastinate when starting the process. Most importantly practice self-discipline for this is essential in making you a successful person.

Successful people are made through the habits they create. By creating good habits and adopting a positive behavior of being goal-oriented, you can accomplish everything you ever want.

Forget the Past

One of the primary purposes of this lifestyle change is you wanting to move on and forget the past. Perhaps you are tired of being overweight, or you are now more concerned about your health that you want to start a new healthy lifestyle. There will always be something that you have tried to forget, urging you to keep moving forward.

The idea of forgetting is right for your brain, for it helps the proper functioning of your memory. Forgetting enables you to construct your life's as you want it and disregarding unnecessary things that contribute to the continuation of your life, allowing you to move towards the future.

One way to do this is to forget your bad habits; for example, if you have been smoking for too long and want to change it. Then forget buying cigarettes anymore. Put it behind you and start looking for a life without smoking. Dive into the repressed stuff and work through it. Look for distraction, focus more on your goals, and always remember that the brain is also built to forget.

Do not let the past become an obstacle to your goals. Do not let it hinder you from achieving the life you want, and do not let it alter your thinking of being fearful of repeating old mistakes.

It Does Not Matter What Everyone Else Thinks

Along the process of building a house, there will always be opinions and suggestions from other people. Like you need to follow the position of walls to avoid lousy omen or perhaps choose a more prominent color of paint or do not make it too fancy to reduce cost.

Eventually, you find yourself drowning in these opinions that you started to contemplate. Most people struggle to grasp the concept of ignoring what other people think. We thrive for that admiration and to please others.

You always act your best when in the presence of others because somehow, you desire admiration or long for it. As soon as this admiration went down and you started to feel being disliked, you begin to scrutinize yourself.

If you wanted to change your lifestyle, make it a point to ignore the things other people say. Try to avoid them as much as you can or better yet keep your distance from people you think can distract you from reaching your lifestyle goals.

Do not allow them to manipulate you into thinking that you are not good enough to create change. People will always talk, the more they get to you, the less you feel about yourself. Figure out ways on how to worry less about them and focus more on your path.

If you wanted to turn yourself around, you need to let go of the fears of being disliked. This will only hold you from achieving the change you always wanted to have and what you are destined for.

- Keep in mind that you have no control over others
- Stay positive and keep focused on your goals
- Practice self-love and self-care
- Remind yourself that you are more than enough

- Forgive and be kind to yourself

Being mindful and caring for other people, especially to your family and friends are essential, but do not allow what other people think to keep you from achieving your dreams.

Let Go of Fear

When you engage in the process of transformation, you need to let go of the thoughts of fear. Emotions reduce your capacity for attracting the things you wanted to have; fear is the strongest. Changing your lifestyle is a complete transformation process.

Sometimes along with the procedure, you get to be anxious, stressed, or even frightened, thinking about the things that might go wrong in the process. It will only hold you back from attaining your dreams and putting you on the right path. The fear of making a mistake is part of being human.

You need to develop a strategy in changing your mindset. Trust the process. Similar to the idea of building a house, you need to trust the depth of its foundation to hold your home still and to keep from breaking amidst natural disasters. If you can put your trust to someone aside from yourself, then you have all the reason to trust yourself more. After all, this journey is all about you.

Communicate Your Wishes with Others

One way of making your process even better is to tell the people around you about the changes you are making. Communicate with others effectively, tell them your limitations and the things you can do. Let them know that you are changing for the best.

For example, if you are in the process of gaining financial independence and saving up money, let your friends know that you may not be able to eat out or join them for money splurges. Let everyone know that you are trying to change for the better and what you are trying to accomplish. By sharing your thoughts and passion, you are making yourself vulnerable, making you more energetic, and help you focus on your path.

This can either deepen your connection to them, build greater trust and respect, or improve your overall social and emotional health. For the people around you, they can build you up. The people around you can be influential and help when they know the purpose of your actions.

The importance of communicating your wishes and other personal thoughts with others is to help others *"step into your shoes"* when making difficult decisions on your behalf. It is better to let others be aware of what you are going through in times of need, and they will be able to help you. Trust them enough that when you need help, they will come running. The people who trust your actions know the reasons behind it. Be grateful for these experiences, and look forward to gaining the lifestyle you always wanted.

This metaphor makes you realize life is mostly in comparison to constructing a house. In creating an experience, you want it similar to building a house. You start with a plan, create your blueprint, write down and take note all of your goals, you become goal-driven, you let go of certain things such as fear and the past, and you hire people that can help surpass the process. Until you can reach the house you have always wanted or the lifestyle you are still dreaming of.

You might need to make some significant changes in your life but for all the right reasons. Trust yourself and strive to become better in life. If you decide to take a step to start now, think about what your life will be like in the next couple of years.

Always remember that the first step of this journey is that first step. Love yourself enough that you will do whatever it takes to create the life you deserve because you deserve it.

Steps to Attract the Life You Want

You have this vision of the life you want. However, you may not know how to achieve it. Start following the steps to find and attract this life. Make it a part of your life.

Follow Your Heart

There is always the popular notion that if you were to put yourself in the situation to choose between your heart and your mind, it is best to follow your heart. For your heart knows better than what you are already thinking. However, this simple phrase is something a lot of people recognize but failed to take action in making a reality.

Instead of deciding based on practical reasons, why not choose to make your goals to follow your heart. The most significant benefit you can have is to stop tieing yourself to the world, to your boss, to your customers, or any other people around you. By following your heart, you stop trying to prove that you are good enough or content enough to support your desires.

Your heart is tender, kind, and guided by meaningful choices. Following your heart and being true to yourself is critical for a useful life. Try to live a more satisfying life by making decisions on what you feel rather than what you think. For instance, in attracting the life you want.

- When you follow your heart, you stop having regrets.
- Find newfound respect for yourself and from those you admire.
- Get to know who you are.
- Learn to love yourself more.
- Learn to trust your intuition.

Tune into the Soul

Some people are guided by their soul, thus creating the world's yoga master, health guru, etc. They consider their soul to instruct them and provide subtle hints that foretold the patterns of their life. To attract the life you want, you need to be guided by your soul's telling.

It takes a lot of deep emotions to check on your connection with your soul because we tend to make decisions based on critical thinking rather than following the calling of their inner soul. You are so full of ideas and judgments about what you should do, or you should not do. People always talk themselves out of the situation and out of their soul's guidance.

It is so much easier to be guided by rational things than to create a connection with your soul. The soul does not speak the same language as you; thus, you need to pay more attention to what your soul is trying to tell you. The soul is about freedom; it cares more about freeing yourself and being true to yourself than anything else. It is entirely different from what the mind is telling you.

Most people who are more tune in to their soul tends to live a simple and frugal life. One of the effects of aligning your life is to let go of all the unnecessary things you used to have. When you learn to align more with your soul each day, life seems to flow more naturally and is less of a struggle.

See the Big Picture

To attract the life you want, you need to see the big picture and focus on what is essential in your life. Look for the benefits that you can get out of completing the process; this way, you become goal-oriented and dream driven. You start doing an activity that could benefit your goals. Moreover, start claiming the life you always dreamed of by revolving most of your action to your goals.

For example, you wanted to gain financial freedom and save money for your retirement. To do this, start creating a system that works for you. Be organized, as this will help you define your goals and set actions on how to achieve them.

Inform the people around you about the things you wanted to accomplish and ask for help when needed. Manage your life effectively by organizing your dreams and taking control of your actions. Let the system you created a guide you towards achieving your goals.

Develop Emotional Self-Mastery

Controlling your emotion is an advantage. Emotions are the most powerful energy you can have. The most successful people develop skills to harness their feelings and do not let these emotions hinder their actions. As you attract the things you want in life, you must find the internal focus of controlling and harnessing your emotions to steer the life of your choosing.

Emotional self-mastery lets you choose the destination of your life, how you will live it, interact with every circumstance, and respond to it. If you know how to control your emotions, you can focus more and reason when making important decisions. Most of the time, your emotions become a factor in ruining some critical events in your life. For example, getting frustrated and disappointed every time you fail. There are circumstances in life that seem too challenging to handle.

Giving up seems to be a better option than to keep trying, and you succumb to your negative emotions. Developing self-mastery will make you strong enough to battle self-defeating traits and habits, which is currently a stumbling block to your joy and happiness.

Align to Your Truth
Aligning your goals to your thoughts, feelings, and actions create a sense of presence and purpose in your life. You become more focused and goal-driven if you know what you want. By staying in touch with who you are, you started to feel confident in reaching your goals. You will create a system that works for you through your thoughts and feelings. These factors will serve as your guide as you go through the process. Do a self-check regularly, keeping emotions intact and head clear because this will align yourself with the truth.

Pay more attention to your current state of life and the things you wanted to achieve. Start creating your system by connecting yourself to your goals by making it more personal. Put your thoughts and emotions in all your actions, and this will make the process easier.

Be aware of environmental influences. The people around you can either contribute or destroy your progress. Negative people can pull you down and disrupt your development, while positive people can help you through motivation. You can impact each other in obvious and subtle ways. The best action to take is by surrounding yourself with people who support you and help you deliver your potential.

Follow Your Intuition
Following your intuition can be a good or bad thing. The best way to think about it is if you do not feel right about something, do not do it. If you feel good about it and think it will work, do it. You will not always have a warm and fuzzy feeling about something. Sometimes, you may have a sour taste for something and cannot figure out why. If you cannot figure out why you are feeling this way, you should follow your feeling. There is always a reason even when it cannot be explained.

Keep Your Head Clear
To attract the life that you want, put your whole focus and determination in your goals. Ignore the things that distract you. Keep your mind clear of all the clutter.

Act
The key to getting what you want in life is to take steps to begin. Now is the best time to start, so what is holding you

back? Do not miss out on the days where you will contemplate the things you have not done or stuck on the what if's. Take the journey of life with no regrets. You may stumble upon hard things, but the only failure in life comes when you do not try. Deciding not to start or procrastinating is worse than failure, for there is no actual failure in life than doing all that you can despite the results.

The only thing that is more daunting than taking action is not making any action at all. Failures are meant to teach you a lesson, just be sure to learn from them. They contain the most significant experiences you could have.

Do something that will ignite your passion and provide the momentum you need. Do whatever it takes to keep your engine going and continue moving forward. If you feel like breaking, pause but never quit, you have more to lose than leaving. Create small steps if you must but never stop moving forward. These small actions are significant and contain the symbolic power to release fear and build self-confidence and the belief that you need.

Keep the faith
Along the process of your lifestyle change, you may find yourself in your worst moments. You have been in situations where you feel like you have lost everything and think that giving up seems to be the best option to take. To battle this, find the ways to cling to your faith when it seems all hope is lost.

Keeping the faith is not only about being healthy. It is about being contented both in times of prosperity and in need. It is about practicing patience during a long wait and process. It is about praying with the audacity to ask God for an answer and keeping your faith intact.

When things get tough, do everything without complaining, and keep steering forward. Do not give in to the temporary pleasure of life, which will result in disrupting your journey. Do not let temporary things console you in feeling better about a specific situation. Instead, handle every hardship with prayer and faith. Ask for guidance from God and help from others to keep moving forward.

In life, hardships are to impart our lessons; if everything were only happy moments, then we would not learn anything. It may seem hard as you go along the process, but keep in mind that it is not impossible to keep your faith intact. It may be with yourself, with other people, or with God, but there is always something to hold on to, especially when your path is becoming rocky. It is sturdy, and God equipped you and the people around you to handle your situation.

Get educated

It is easy to ask others about how to do things. However, you will never learn by always asking. The best thing to do is to learn how to do it for yourself. Take classes, visit Udemy, or watch YouTube videos. Do what it takes to learn about what you do not know about.

Keep learning

Life is a learning process. You will never stop learning. As you are educating yourself to do something, you are learning a new skill. These new skills can be carried with you your entire life.

Network

Networking is essential for a successful career. It does not matter if you are looking for work or self-employed. Creating your own network will help you grow to success. Use your system to draw in business and customers.

The Path to Begin Designing Your Lifestyle

You design the future. It is not written in stone. It is what you make of it. If you work at a regular job, you may not call the shots. However, you do call the shots and create your own future.

Remember That You Call the Shots

The most important thing to remember is you have choices. You make the decisions; you call the shots! Sometimes some moments prompt you to decide because *"you have no choice."* A lot of people often say it for all types of reasons, from a common problem to a dilemma or small fixes.

One of the common examples for this is an employee staying with a job he hates only because of the high salary. If you were to ask why he keeps in the same situation, he would only say, *"I have no choice,"* which is both condemning and distressful. While these people think they are in conditions with no options, there will always be choices. Decide that you want to live a vibrant life and accept the fact that it may look different from other people.

There are things that you cannot change, and you do not have a choice as they say. You do have a choice on how you react in every situation you face. For instance, if you were working in a job that you dislike just for the reason of gaining enough income to support your family, you do have a choice in how you react—perhaps creating a goal that serves as a diversion of your hardships. This way, you will start to feel positive about your job.

Sometimes, you may seem to forget that you have a choice because the circumstances are daunting. They become strong enough to overpower you to the point where life looks like another season of a series of unfortunate events. You see yourself facing no other options. Either way, you can react helplessly or continue to suffer from your problems.

Keep in mind, you have your own life, and it is yours and no one else's. It is part of your nature to live with choices in life. You are unique and talented in a particular way. You have the opportunity to live the life you always wanted and experience the things that bring you joy.

Get a Little Selfish

After realizing that you have choices, the next thing to do is spend a little time with yourself and figure out what your options will look like. Get down on being selfish, not with others, but with yourself. Self-care is more important to keep your emotional and physical well-being intact. There are a lot of ways to practice how to be selfish.

For example, you are saying no to your friends for a night out in exchange for getting more sleep since you had an all-nighter last night. Being selfish is defined as being concerned with your personal growth and simply means putting yourself first.

In attracting the life you want, being selfish creates the blueprint that helps you narrow down the things you ought to do. For instance, you love deep sea fishing, so you decided to live in a coastal place. Being selfish means to sit down, do some soul searching, and figure out precisely what you want during your time on this earth.

Embrace Change and Just Do It
Once you figure out the things you want to do in life and how your life will look, it is time just to do it. Take the step to start, take action, and start making the life you always dreamed of. It might seem scary at first, but this should not stop you from taking each step and moving forward.

Embracing change in life is essential to your growth as an individual and for you to become a better person. Change never seems natural or easy for most people. You either accept it gradually or repel it away. However, change is inevitable, and taking it contributes to your self-development.

In achieving lifestyle change, there is not a better day to start making actions than now. Start small if you need to and make minor changes if you must. Change does not happen overnight, and the lifestyle you want will not be handed to you in a silver platter, but instead, you have to work for it.

The point is to get started and start making things happen. Along the process, you will gain momentum and will likely experience more significant changes and growth in your life.

The Best Way to Create a Vision You Want in Life

You need to have a clear vision of the future. What do you want in life? Where do you see yourself? Envision yourself in the future and bring to you what you really want.

Why You Need a Vision

It is the concept of *"if you do not know where you are going, you will likely end up nowhere."* The importance of vision is to communicate your goals and values. It is similar to our very own sense of sight as it is used for us to be able to see the things around us. It sets out the path of your actions towards your lifelong dreams.

You envision the things you wanted to do and have in the future. It creates a mental picture of the outcome of life you wish to have, and it is keen to help you make that outcome a reality. It is a picture of tangible results, and it inspires you to create action. You need to have a vision in life to build your plans, objectives, and goals. This will then be carried out by your activities and supported by the resources around you.

It is a powerful toolset out to pull your ideas and resources to make change happen. It creates the energy that you need for you to commit to your goals. The reality is if you do not set your visions, you will allow other people to do it for you.

How Do You Create a Life Vision?
Have patience in creating and developing your vision. Nothing successful happened overnight. The process of envisioning your life and directing the path of your life requires a full amount of time and reflection. You need to incorporate vision and perspective and apply logic to your planning.

The best version of your intuition comes from your dreams, hopes, and aspirations. It reflects your values and ideas and ultimately provide the energy and motivation to help you strengthen your commitment to developing the possibilities of your life.

To create the vision that you want. Ask yourself first the following possible questions:

- What do you want to achieve in life?
- What are your goal and dreams?

- What difference from your current situation do you want to happen?
- What kind of lifestyle do you want to have in the future?
- How long are you going to work for your goals?

Use these questions to guide you in creating your visions. Set out plans to align with your objectives and use these specific objectives as your inspiration to keep moving forward. Always remember your life serves to have a purpose; your time on earth should not be wasted with ordinary things. Make your life significant by creating the path less taken and be an inspiration to others by obtaining your goals. Not all people become memorable, but a handful of people become the person they wanted to be because of their visions.

What Do You Want?

Most often, this is the easiest and deceptively simple question people ask but is always the hardest to answer. Letting yourself explore your deepest desire can be frightening. Sometimes, you might not find the time to consider something as fanciful as your dreams.

Usually, what happens is you have been pulled by the strong current of reality that limits your time to dream, but it is essential to remind yourself that a fulfilled life does not usually happen by chance, but by your version of goals. Keep in mind that there is no best time to fulfill your dream but now start reaching for it and make your vision happen.

It is beneficial to ask these kinds of questions, as this will help you discover the opportunities of what you want out of life. To do this, contemplate every aspect of your life, personal and professional, tangible, and intangible. Nurture what you have in life. Take care of your relationships with your family and friends. Respect your career and see success.

You may also add health and quality of life but also do not neglect fun and enjoyment. You need to understand that you can create the experience you want, and you are more powerful than you think. You just need to learn how to do it. There is not a perfect formula for you to succeed. Most people fail at first. Those you see success will not wait for tomorrow. They will act now and get it done. The faster you move, the quicker you can see growth in yourself and your business.

If You Want a Different Result, Change Your Thinking

What can you do to begin changing? Of all the things discussed in this chapter, it mainly highlighted one specific phrase, and that is to *"Keep moving forward."* This phrase has been mentioned in several paragraphs and bears the most significance in every person with a goal. Hearing these words make a man more than motivated.

For life will always pull you off the board; there will always be moments that you will end up slacking and contemplate giving up, but the purpose of this chapter is not to turn the tides more on you but rather help you get on board again. You just need to create a vision and start changing your behaviors.

Bear in mind that you have to be more than willing to change your behavior if you want a different life. You have to take all the necessary risks to get where you wanted to be.

If you already took the step to start and started heading towards the right direction, now is the time to plan more and keep moving forward faster. Remember, you are only a passenger in your life's journey, and you will be thrown off board multiple times. It is up to you how to get back sailing, but you do, however, have a variety of choices and resources at you again; its either you react positively or succumbed to the waves of negativity.

You need to do one thing differently today than what you did yesterday. Commit your whole effort and time for every aspect of your life. Decide to make changes and take one step close to your dream. Make each day an opportunity and if you find yourself failing, start over but never give up. Start the process; you will realize by controlling your thoughts, your visualizations, and your actions, it is much easier to get what you want!

Conclusion

There has been a lot of information I have given you in throughout this book. Thank you for taking this journey with me. I hope you could get value out of the things I have introduced. Being successful is a choice. It is a choice you make to be free from all your debts and see that freedom and the end of the tunnel.

Jeff Bezos found financial freedom when he founded Amazon. Before Amazon, he had his share of debt and hardship. I do not think I need to tell you what happened with his success. Bezos is worth over $116 billion and is the richest man in the world. It is possible to get out of debt and start to work towards having everything you ever wanted through financial freedom, as Bezos did.

The internet is full of successful people and success stories. Take the time to research them and use them as an inspiration. Each one of them started out the same as you and I. There is nothing different about how we begin our journey. The most significant difference is how we react to the situations we are handed.

In the beginning, I talked about the different generations. When you search for success stories, look at the age they come from. You will find that there are success stories from every generation. Therefore, it does not matter what generation you come from. You can still obtain financial freedom.

Put in the work, follow the strategies I have given you, listen to other successful people, follow your dreams, and make it happen. The choice is yours, and no one else's.

Thank you for going on this journey to financial freedom with me and thank you for purchasing this book. Use it as a guidebook for traveling this long road. Share with your friends, families, and anyone you meet. You are not in this alone. Today, anything is possible.

www.ingramcontent.com/pod-product-compliance
Lightning Source LLC
Chambersburg PA
CBHW071400210526
45465CB00001B/187